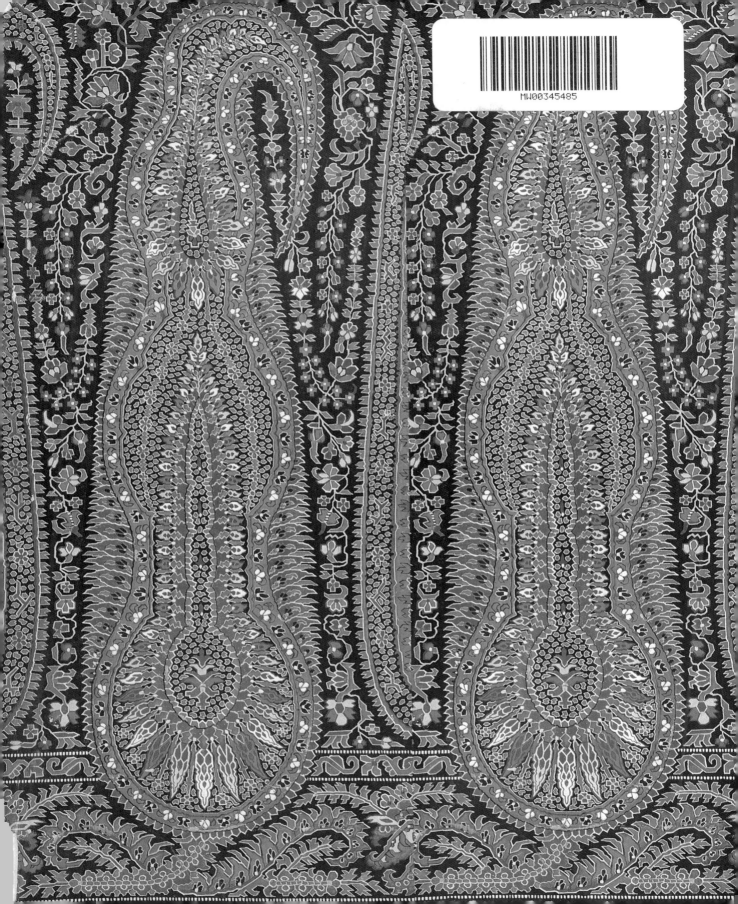

The Paisley Pattern

THE OFFICIAL ILLUSTRATED HISTORY

The Paisley Pattern

VALERIE REILLY

RICHARD DREW   GLASGOW

First published 1987 by
RICHARD DREW PUBLISHING LIMITED
6 Clairmont Gardens, Glasgow G3 7LW
Scotland.

© Renfrew District Council Museums
and Art Galleries Service 1987

The Publisher acknowledges financial
assistance from the Scottish Arts
Council.

British Library Cataloguing in Publication Data

Reilly, Valerie
    The Paisley pattern.
    1. Textile design — Scotland
    I. Title
    746'.09411   NK8845

ISBN 0-86267-193-0

Designed by James W. Murray
Typeset by Swains Glasgow
Illustration reproduction by Swains Edinburgh
Printed and bound in Scotland by
Blantyre Printing & Co. Ltd.

Contents

Introduction

From the middle years of the eighteenth century a new garment began to enter the world of fashion in Europe, initially in Britain and then somewhat later in France and the other Continental countries. It is ironic that it became an essential part of the wardrobe of fashionable ladies because in the country of its origin, Kashmir, it had been a garment worn by men. These pieces of richly woven, soft goats' down fabric had long been highly prized by even the princes of Kashmir, and they soon came to be equally appreciated by the women of Europe. The shawl, with its distinctive teardrop pattern, had arrived.

They were brought to Europe by the East India Company, and the only obstacle to the ownership of one of the Kashmir shawls was their tremendous cost. So around 1780 manufacturers in Edinburgh and Norwich began producing shawls '. . . in imitation of the Indian'. Other major centres of production, such as Paris and Vienna, took up the shawl during the first decade of the nineteenth century as did Paisley, the town whose name has become virtually synonymous with the shawl in the English-speaking world.

As a fashion the shawl lasted for almost a century, simply because it was able to adapt to the changes in the fashions it was worn with. The first peak for the shawl occurred around 1800 when fashion mimicked late Greek and Roman costume, with waistlines just below the bust and very straight, light-coloured dresses. The drape of the long stole-like shawls beautifully complemented the dresses, while at the same time adding a splash of colour.

The early imitations were woven by totally different techniques

Kashmir shawl c 1800.

· 7 ·

from the Kashmirs, allowing the European products greatly to under-cut the price of the original imported shawls. Ladies bought the imitation shawls in ever increasing numbers, encouraging the various manu-facturing centres to turn more and more looms to their production. Paisley, searching for a new product, because of a depression in its late eighteenth-century mainstay of silk, was more active than some other centres, in particular Edinburgh, in pursuing the new industry. In fact so determinedly did the town enter the field of shawl production, that by the 1840s Paisley was virtually a one-industry town. Evidence for this can be found in the suffering and misery caused whenever there occurred one of the periodic trade depressions. These were particularly bad in the 1840s with eventually the whole town going bankrupt. However the trade enjoyed a revival, partly due to the introduction of the new Jacquard loom, and partly due to another change in ladies' fashions.

The 1840s saw the development of the crinoline skirt for which a new size of shawl, called the plaid, was produced. It became the most

Typical shawl made in Paisley c 1840.

Shawl of the 1840s showing intertwining pines and bright colours.

typical outdoor garment of the early- to mid-Victorian period. Paisley was by this time mass-producing shawls and plaids to such an extent that other manufacturing centres were eclipsed. Drapers' shops would offer to their customers a selection of 'Paisleys'. The word Paisley became firmly fixed in the Victorian mind in association with both the shawl and the pattern it bore.

Finally, however, fashion took a turn which the shawls could not follow. Crinoline skirts were replaced by bustles with which the plaids made an ugly combination. Soon they were replaced by other outerwear such as capes or jackets. The manufacturers who had made the shawls had to turn to other products to survive. As a consequence, the Paisley textile industry which had clung to its handlooms, was all but wiped out in the face of competition from the power looms by then in use everywhere else. Small numbers of looms were kept in work, more as a social service to their weavers than for commercial reasons. Since 1942 Paisley has had no vestige of the weaving industry which once sent its name ringing to the four corners of the world.

The 'Paisley' Pattern

Myth and legend surround the origins of the so-called 'Paisley' pattern. The one sure fact is that it did not originate in Paisley. Various natural objects have been claimed as the inspiration for the pattern which the Paisley weavers termed the 'pine'. It has been likened to the fruit of the mango tree (and indeed in India today it is often called the mango pattern), and also to a kind of gourd or pitcher plant found in India. However the consensus of opinion tends towards regarding the 'pine' as a representation of the growing shoot of the date palm (similar in appearance to the tight curl of a young bracken frond as it begins to grow). It seems to have originated in ancient Chaldea (Babylon) and from there it began its spread into both India and prehistoric Europe.

The Chaldeans regarded the date palm as the tree of life, so necessary was it to their mode of existence. It provided food, wine, thatch, wood, paper and string, and therefore it meant prosperity and plenty. The 'pine', as a representation of the male part of the palm, came to be symbolic of the renewal of life itself. The symbol was incorporated into textiles, embroideries, tiles and carvings, and flourished as an important element of early Indian art. In Europe traces of the symbol can be seen in the decorative arts of many cultures including the well-known Celtic art. But in Europe the arts of these cultures died away under the influence of the Classical motifs of Greece and Rome.

Shawls incorporating the motif began to be woven in Kashmir, a northern Indian province, late in the seventeenth century. The early motif was much more delicate and naturalistic than the nineteenth-century Paisley 'pine', but the embryo of it was there in the outline

The Desborough Mirror is one of Britain's finest pieces of Celtic Art. It clearly shows the curls and swirls which were the roots of the Paisley pattern.

shape. A shawl of this type can be seen in the painting of Abdullah Qutb-Shah.

Early in the eighteenth century the motif had been conventionalised into a tightly-packed pyramid of flowers above a 'vase', a style influenced by Indo-Persian art. The name given to these motifs, still used in India, is būtā (or boteh) literally meaning 'flower'. In the middle of the century the motif acquired a yet more formal outline which increasingly tended to bend over at the top. From 1770 onwards this būtā took on more and more of the shape of a curling pointed leaf filled with floral pattern, the colours being nearly always primary.

European copiers of this design in the nineteenth century understood little or nothing of the Oriental symbolism. The būtā therefore was adapted and developed to cater for Western tastes, acquiring new names such as the 'pine', or the 'tadpole' (in France) or the 'little onion' (in Vienna).

Trying to date historical textiles by means of a stylistic chronology is always difficult. Weavers generally tend to be conservative in outlook and are usually reluctant to depart from a tried and tested success. The old designs continue to be made alongside newly introduced ones, and

This painting (c 1670) shows Abdullah Qutb-Shah of Golconda wearing an early style of Kashmir shawl.

One of two known fragments of a very early Kashmir shawl. It is 17th century in date.

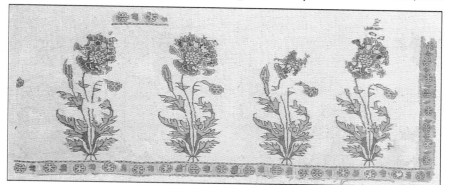

will sometimes even outlive them. Despite this, some of the developments of the 'pine' pattern can be followed during the years when Europe made shawls '. . . in imitation of the Indian'. Western designers absorbed the Indian taste for angular forms and bright colours, but also exercised their talents showing much imagination and invention. The earliest imitations, due mainly to the limited technical capabilities of the looms, do not generally have the true 'pine' pattern. Instead they have narrow borders of floral or seaweed-like patterning. The first Paisley-made shawls had 'a perverse-looking, wry-necked sprig, in one colour — generally green — or made up of little bars of various colours, like so many chips of painted wood built into the required shapeless form.' Paisley began to produce shawls with the 'pine' pattern around about 1814. These first 'pines' were infilled with the mosaic style men-

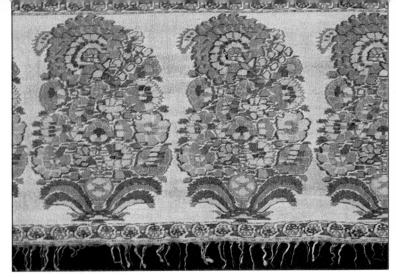

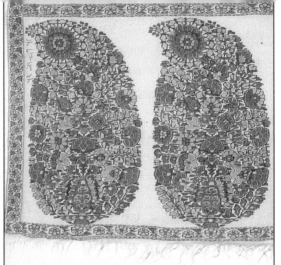

Early 18th century 'vase of flowers' style Kashmir shawl.

Late 18th century Kashmir shawl which still retains the stylised 'vase', but which has attained the more familiar 'Paisley' shape.

Early imitation shawl of silk and cotton, c 1810.

tioned above, but gradually they became more floral, being filled with flowers, buds, stalks and leaves. The pines began to be divided lengthways and the spaces in between them filled with a 'light spray figuring called the wreath'. Also a belt of pattern called the laurel appeared around the pine but exactly following its outline.

By the 1840s French taste was all the rage. The 'pine' had for a short time been supplanted by novelty shawls such as those made of damask, angola or Canton crêpe, but made a revival with new features. It bent and twisted in all directions and was generally drawn in groups of two or three with intertwining outlines. This was probably the best period for the pattern. The 'pines' flowed naturally with the drape of the material they decorated and the colours were bright and clear.

With the introduction of the Jacquard loom, designs could be woven that were much more complex than those of the earlier shawls, and according to one shawl historian 'the design of a plaid became a glorious medley of curves'. The tendency, apparent from the beginning of the shawl era, for the pattern to become more elaborate and fill more and more of the surface, became more marked after the 1840s. The Victorians seemed to abhor a plain surface, and as a consequence the pines swirled and elongated until they often stretched right from corner to centre. However, this trend could also go too far, producing shawls which, because of their fussiness, are really not at all pleasing to the modern eye. Fortunately there were many more of the good designs, and apart from a brief interlude about 1853 when a fern-like pattern called 'Fanny's Fern' became popular, the 'pine' reigned supreme until the end of the Paisley-shawl industry.

The 'Paisley pattern' has, of course, flourished in the years since 1870. It has been used in almost every branch of textile manufacture from the embroidery on silk underwear, to the pattern of high-quality carpeting. In the second decade of this century it enjoyed a revival in the United States with a New York firm hand-printing lengths of silk with designs copied from actual Paisley shawls. The silk, it was advised, would make handsome blouses or evening gowns, but would be particularly good for the lining of one's opera cloak. In the 1960s in particular there was a great vogue for anything and everything in 'Paisley'. It was said at the time; 'Addicts can now wear Paisley from hat to shoe: they can sit on Paisley covered sofas, and sleep on Paisley beds, and even cover their husbands in Paisley.' Other articles decorated with the Paisley pattern included ties, dresses, dressing-gowns, jackets, underwear, furnishing, wallpapers, curtains, mugs, hats, umbrellas and gloves. The pattern never really completely goes out of fashion, and it is likely that this very day, you could walk into any high-street chain store and purchase at least one article in Paisley pattern.

Selection of contemporary items of Paisley pattern gathered together for an exhibition held in Paisley Museum in 1969.

Three-quarter plaid, c 1820. The spaces between the border pines are beginning to be infilled with pattern.

Design, c 1840, from the pattern book of John Morgan & Co., of Paisley.

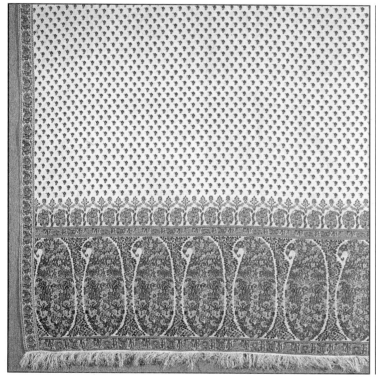

All–over pattern plaid, c 1860. No plain surface is left in this example

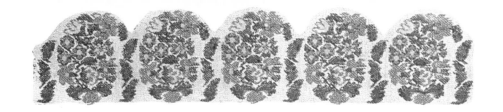

Shawl Production

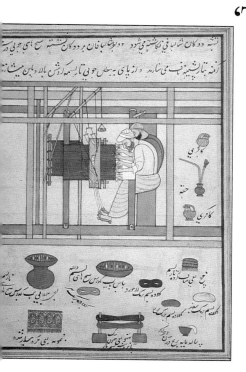

A mid-19th century native painting of a Kashmir shawl loom and weaving implements.

'The "Paisley Shawl" was ... an attempt to produce in the loom the effects which, in the Indian Cashmere Shawl, were produced by the needle.' But there was in fact more than one production method used on Kashmir shawls. One type was completely composed of patchwork with many small pieces of pictorial embroidery carefully arranged, and almost invisibly sewn together. The true Kashmir shawl, however, was woven on a simple frame loom. In such shawls, unlike the European weaving, the weft threads do not run across the complete width of the fabric. Instead they are sewn in, using a needle-like shuttle, concentrating on one separate patch of colour at a time. This is known as the twill-tapestry technique, since it is the same method as is used in Europe to weave tapestries. It is long and laborious and a true Kashmir shawl might take the weaver two or three years to complete. A third type of Indian shawl consisted of small sections of twill-tapestry woven cloth sewn together patchwork-fashion. This produced a shawl more quickly since many weavers could work simultaneously on the patches, but the results were always inferior to the true needle-and-loom-woven Kashmir shawl.

It was these Kashmir products that the European manufacturers had to copy and, if they were to sell large numbers, undercut in price. Designing shawls to look like the Indian originals proved no great difficulty. The designers could take their inspiration directly from original Kashmir shawls, from other European imitations, or from details of shawls specially printed for the purpose. For example, there was a book published in France, called *Le Cachemirien,* showing the designs of

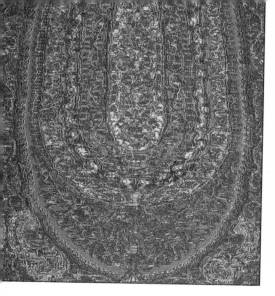

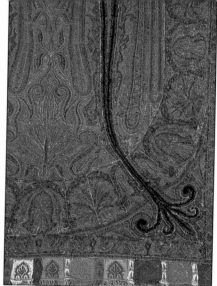

Reverse of a twill-tapestry woven Kashmir shawl, clearly showing the characteristic lines of transposed colours.

Kashmir shawl of the 1850s, which is twill-tapestry woven but pieced together in patchwork style.

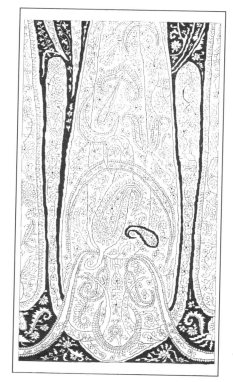

Page from Le Cachemirien, *illustrating a Lahore-made shawl belonging to the Duchesse de Berry.*

Indian shawls belonging to the French nobility. Of course each designer also had to be a student of Indian art and design in general, and also enough of a weaving technician to understand the limitations of what could and could not be produced on the European looms.

Having gained inspiration, from whatever source, the designer's first step was to produce a preliminary sketch of a quarter or a half of the shawl in miniature. This was usually done in pencil or India ink and was rarely coloured. Detailed drawings of various sections such as borders, corners and centres would then be made. All these would be passed on to a colourer who transferred them onto oiled paper (a semi-transparent paper where large blocks of colour could be painted onto the back and fine details painted on the front). Finally a draughtsman took the coloured designs and transferred them to a form of graph paper. In the weaving industry this is properly known as 'point-paper' and in it each small square represents one crossing of the warp and weft threads in the finished article. This process necessarily enlarged the design, and a completed point-paper design for a plaid could be of a size to cover the floor of a large room.

In matters of professionalism in pattern design, however, it was not Paisley but France that was the leader. Under the rule of Napoleon Bonaparte, leading artists were commissioned to produce variations of the Kashmir pattern more in conformity with French taste. And it was French taste that came to dominate the trade in Europe, as by the 1840s British manufacturers were imitating the French imitations of the Kashmir shawls. In fact much of the evidence suggests that Paisley did not bother to produce many of its own designs, at least until British opposition had all but been destroyed. Frequent complaints from Norwich and Edinburgh speak of the way Paisley 'pirated' their designs. There is even a claim that Paisley manufacturers kept agents at the dockside in London to await each new shipment of Kashmir shawls. These agents would take tracings of the latest designs and rush them to Paisley so that within a week or so the manufacturers would have copies heading back for London, greatly undercutting the originals in price (£20 as opposed to £200 or more). This claim seems nonsensical, as it would take weeks rather than days to produce point-paper designs, set up a warp, lash a harness and weave a shawl, quite apart from the fact that it would probably take at least a week to transport the designs from London to Paisley, given the state of the roads at the period when this system is said to have been in operation, about 1812. Complaints about Paisley's pirating of designs reached a peak in the early 1840s and eventually the Government were persuaded, by the main British rivals Norwich, to allow the protection of designs for three, six or nine months under the patents system.

In producing imitation Indian shawls however, there was another factor to consider, besides that of the surface pattern. The main distinctive feature of the true Kashmir shawls was their feel. The beautifully soft wool of which these shawls were made was unique, and none of the substitutes tried by the European manufacturers were found to be adequate. This wool, of which the Kashmir weavers had a monopoly, came from a Central Asian species of goat (capra hircus). Most prized was the

Pencil sketch showing a quarter of a plaid design, signed and dated in Paisley in 1866.

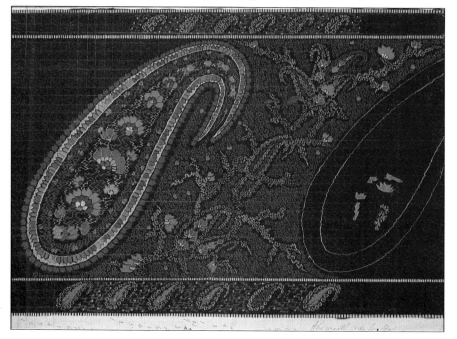

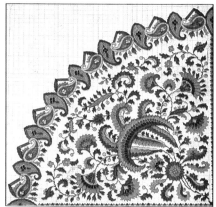

Pattern detail worked out for a medallion centre shawl, c 1820.

Border detail taken from a Paisley shawl manufacturer's pattern book, c 1840.

This 'Shaul Goat from Boutan' was painted in 1779.

Point paper pattern for a 'leafy' shawl border, c 1840.

Point paper was specially printed in Paisley for the weavers to use.

underfleece grown as protection against the intense cold of the goat's natural habitat, the high Himalayas. The underfleece (known as pashmina) is shed at the beginning of each summer, and was collected from the rocks and thorn bushes. The best quality came from the highest and therefore coldest places, but was somewhat limited in supply. As a supplement domesticated goats were also kept. These domesticated goats each produced about two pounds (900 g) of down every year, which was

Kashmir shawl of the mid-19th century, showing the influence of European taste.

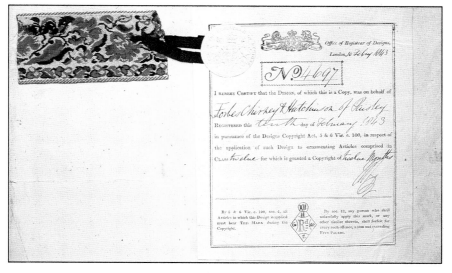

Forbes, Chirney & Hutchison, a firm who made both woven and printed shawls in Paisley, patented this sample of a woven border in 1843.

enough to weave one shawl approximately 4 feet 6 inches (1.4 m) square.

The native regard for the goats is shown in a treaty of 1846 between the British Government and Gulab Singh who controlled the Vale of Kashmir after the First Sikh War. In it, as a token of British supremacy, he promised to present Britain annually with one horse, twelve perfect shawl goats (six male and six female) and three pairs of Kashmir shawls.

Attempts were made on various occasions to naturalise the goat in

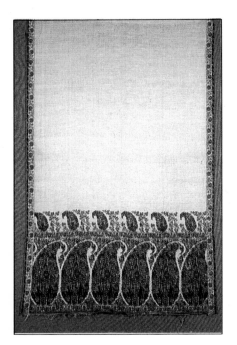

This early three-quarter plaid, c 1815, was made with a warp of silk, but the pattern weft threads are of cotton and wool.

Europe, especially as the Board of Agriculture suggested in 1808 that successful naturalisation 'would offer a richer prize to our manufacturers than the acquisition of the golden fleece'. In 1812, therefore, a British vet named William Moorcroft sought and obtained permission to lead an expedition into Western Tibet on behalf of the East India Company. They brought back fifty goats, but for some reason the males and females were shipped separately to Britain. Unfortunately the females were lost at sea, and of the males only four survived the journey to Scotland where they too soon died. A similar expedition was launched by the French in 1818. They managed to capture more than 1,200 goats in West Kazakhstan, of which only some two or three hundred survived the journey to France. Two pairs were brought to England and by 1828 the herd had increased to 27, yielding just enough wool for three shawls. In sharp contrast to the Indian domesticated goats, those reared in Essex only produced between two and four ounces (55 to 115 g) of down each year. The manufacturers gave up any thought of large-scale goat rearing when it was discovered that the quality of the cashmere was slowly deteriorating. Cold as the British winters were, they were not cold enough to stimulate the goats to produce the high-quality downy underfleece.

In the absence of the original wool, the European manufacturers conducted many experiments to try and simulate the feel of the cashmere yarn. Before 1820, no woollen yarn produced in Britain was fine enough, yet strong enough, to stand the strain of being lifted by the harness if used as warp thread. So substitute yarns of silk combined with wool or cotton were used instead. The warp yarn for the best Paisley shawls came from Amiens, and consisted of cashmere wool spun around a silk core to give the woollen softness and the silken strength. This was used together with a weft of botany worsted which was spun from fine Australian wool and sent from the spinning mills in Bradford to Paisley by way of Liverpool and the Clyde. In an attempt to reproduce the Kashmir fabric a Yorkshire company produced 'Thibet cloth', a twilled fabric of fine worsted yarn, but again it would not stand up to the rigours of the harness and so it was used for the centres of shawls with sewn-on borders.

Spinning techniques were gradually improved and eventually a cashmere yarn was spun which could be used in harness weaving. In 1834 the Board of Manufacturers had one section of its annual competitions reserved solely for shawls woven of cashmere spun in Scotland. Since the fleece had to be imported, however, genuine cashmere always remained very expensive.

For the general run of Paisley shawls it is possible to see phases in the use of different types and qualities of yarn. In the early period there was almost always a high proportion of silk in the shawl, usually a silk warp,

with silk, wool and cotton (or combinations thereof) used as weft threads. It was not until the 1830s that all-wool shawls appeared and they remained popular through into the 1840s, though shawls of other fabrics did continue to be made. It was in the 1850s and 1860s however that the greatest variety of different types were made. Plaids appeared made completely of silk, and these lustrous garments must have commanded a high price on the fashion market. There were also plaids purely of wool or of cotton, and contrary to expectations an all-cotton plaid is not necessarily of low quality. There are, in fact, some cotton plaids as good as, if not better than, their woollen counterparts. The quality of the shawl seems to depend more on the tightness of the weave than on the yarn it is made of. A loosely-woven shawl or plaid uses much less yarn than a tightly-woven one of the same size, and can therefore be sold more cheaply. The later period of the plaid also saw many examples of cotton and wool used in the same garment and these seem to fall into the medium-quality range. It seems to be very rare in these latter years for silk to be mixed with other fibres. Despite their many experiments with yarns the manufacturers were always considered to have failed to copy the feel of Indian shawls. In her correspondence with the Paisley manufacturer John Morgan, Lady Maxwell of Pollok speaks of lending him sample Indian shawls so that he can try to get his copies closer in feel to the real thing.

After selecting the yarn to be used, the next step was to dye it in the required colours. There seems to have been little in the way of a dyeing industry in Paisley in the early years of the nineteenth century and yarns were probably brought into the town ready dyed. However this had

All-wool shawl, c 1830.

All-over pattern shawl, c 1860, made completely from silk.

In this good-quality, tightly-woven plaid of the 1860s no trace of the (vertical) warp threads can be seen between the closely beaten-up wefts (which run left to right).

In this more loosely woven example of the same period, the vertical warp threads can be seen, particularly in the pink areas.

Plaid, c 1860. The colours which are most likely to be aniline are the purple of the main pattern, and the yellow and blue of the fringe area.

This compartment-centre plaid, c 1855, shows where red warp threads have strayed into the area which was meant to be white.

probably proved uneconomical by the time shawl production went ahead on a massive scale in the middle of the century. The Paisley dyers seem to have quickly got the processes down to a fine art. The dyeing book of Mr James Barclay gives recipes for dyeing wool, cotton, jute and linen, with various dyestuffs of vegetable and mineral origin. These include such exotic names as Copperass, Prussiate, Shumach, seaflower bled, Pearl ash, saffron, 'malachite' green, pink crystals and Congo Orange along with commoner dyes such as chrome, iron, lime, logwood, extract of indigo and whiting. These natural substances gave pleasing subtle colours, but in the 1850s they began to be superseded by the chemically formed aniline dyes. Shawls and plaids of the 1850s and 1860s often exhibit combinations of the harsh and garish colours produced by aniline dyes.

The dyers showed their skill whenever warps had to be dyed before weaving could commence. In particular this applied to the multi-coloured borders known as tail-pieces, and in the compartments at the centres of two- or four-colour shawls. A specially constructed frame would be used to hold the warp, exposing only the appropriate sections for dyeing. This required great skill since the smallest inaccuracy would show up as a fault in the finished shawl. It was because the results achieved were so good that Paisley latterly became famed as a dyeing centre.

Having got a design and yarn, the next stage was to set up the loom ready to begin weaving. This job was generally not done by the weaver himself but by one or more specialists who travelled from loomshop to loomshop to do this work. A warper would wind the chosen yarn into the correct lengths for the loom. In many cases, as we have already seen, this would be done before the dyeing process. The beamer would then take the warp and set it onto the beams of the loom. He might be assisted by a drawer to draw each separate warp thread through the eyelet holes of the heddles. The loom was now prepared for the harness to be set in readiness. Two types of loom are known to have been used in Paisley for the shawl-weaving trade. In the early years of the nineteenth century, the drawloom was the only type capable of producing curvilinear designs. The harness of a drawloom was attended to by a 'flower-lasher'. Taking the point-paper design approved by the manufacturer, he would read along each line of the pattern and tie the harness cords in the appropriate groupings, allowing the loom to pick up irregular sequences of warp threads in order to produce the pattern. When the drawloom was replaced by the Jacquard, the 'flower-lasher' gave way to the 'card-cutter'. The cards were cut by a 'piano' machine. Again following each line of the point-paper design, the cutter would use combinations of the ten keys on the machine to cut holes in the correct places on the cards. The cards were then laced into a continuous band and passed

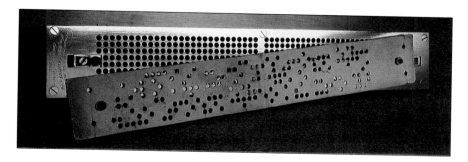

Card, and cutting plate, for use in conjunction with a Jacquard loom.

to the weaver ready for his machine. Preparing a set of cards for a Jacquard must have been a time-consuming job when one considers that it might take as many as 424,000 cards for one plaid.

The drawloom was basically a handloom with the addition of an overhead harness. This was worked by an operative, additional to the weaver himself, known as a drawboy (though it must be pointed out that they were not all male, 'drawgirls' are known to have existed). The drawboy's job was to pull a cord, called a simple, at the side of the loom. This had the effect of raising one or more harness threads, and thereby the warp threads running through the eyelet holes (or mails) of the heddles. Below each harness thread hung a lead weight designed to keep the web taut. When the selected warp threads had been raised by the drawboy (an action which caused him to lift anything between 6 oz (170 g) and 3 lbs (1.4 kg) of lead weight) the weaver would use his poukin pin to push a shuttle filled with a pirn of weft thread through the resultant gaps in the warp. To avoid the drawboy having to lift greater weights the shawls were woven face downwards, and the weaver would only see a confused mass of floating threads on the reverse. It was therefore the job of the drawboy to ensure that the simples were pulled in correct sequence, and the correct colour weft was used. Mistakes would not be noticed until the shawl came off the loom anything up to two weeks later. It is sad to reflect that many of these (on average) 10-year-old children might receive beatings for a few moments inattention in what was often a 12-hour working day.

Because of the inherent deficiencies of the drawloom, attempts had been made as far back as 1728 to replace the drawboy with a mechanical system. The invention was not perfected, however, until about 1800 when a French weaver named Jacquard managed to raise harness threads using a mechanism activated by perforated cards. It worked by a system of needles coming up against each card. If there was a hole, the needle went through and a harness thread was raised; if there was no perforation the mechanism was not activated. The new loom was slow to be adopted in Britain where it was resisted by the workers, since it was at first seen as a method by which the manufacturers could reduce their

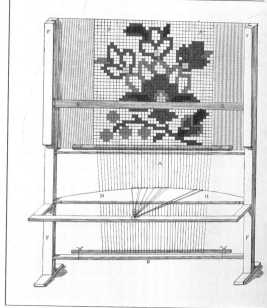

The flower-lasher's frame allowed him to read off the point paper design and tie the harness cords to produce the correct pattern on the loom.

Silk-woven portrait of M. Jacquard.

workforce. However, from instructions written into some of the manu-facturers' pattern books, we know that a few Jacquards were in use in Paisley by the mid-1820s. They must have made a good impression as they had greatly increased by the 1830s, and Paisley has the credit of being probably the earliest weaving centre in Britain to under-take large-scale Jacquard work. It was probably one of the factors which allowed Paisley to outstrip its more laggardly competitors, by dominating the mass market.

The job of the weaver, though eased by the assistance of the warper and beamer etc., was not without its complications. Having set up the loom, but before beginning to weave, the weaver had to dress the web. This was a method of strengthening the warp threads by spreading on a starch paste, and then wafting it with a goose-quill fan to dry it (it was from supplying starch to the Paisley weavers that Brown and Polson branched out into the cornflour industry). During the actual weaving, accuracy was all-important. Each weft thread (or 'shot') put across the warp had to be pushed snugly up against its predecessor, a process known as 'beating up'. If the weave was allowed to become too tight, or too loose, the pattern of the shawl would be distorted or destroyed.

This Jacquard loom is preserved in Paisley Museum, where a new harness has recently been fitted.

Additionally the manufacturers would not accept a shawl or plaid varying more than a quarter of an inch (6 mm) from the stipulated length (which could leave the weaver greatly out of pocket). The closeness of the weave would be checked regularly using the 'web glass'. This was a small lens in a brass mounting, through which the weaver could count the number of weft threads appearing in a given length of cloth. The first shawl to be woven on any particular web would be cut and taken to the warehouse for inspection. Only if it was approved could the weaver go ahead and weave the rest of the web. With the Jacquard loom, it was often the practice to weave a second web of shawls in a different colour combination, particularly if the pattern proved to be popular. This made the best possible use of the set of pattern cards, which could be very expensive to produce. There was a Government tax on the card used, which could send the price of a set up to about £100. The manufacturers complained bitterly over this as they felt it gave a distinct advantage to their continental competitors who had no such tax to face.

The processes involved in finishing the shawl were almost as long as those leading up to the weaving, and again the work was done by specialists rather than by the weaver himself. In fact from design to finish, about a dozen specialists were involved in the production of a shawl. When the shawl reached the warehouse, the back had to be clipped to remove all the surplus floating threads. In the early days of the industry

Reverse side of an 1830s shawl, after undergoing the clipping process.

Here we can see the effective re-use of a set of Jacquard cards. These three 1850s plaids are almost identical, except that the two outer examples have different patterns immediately above the fringe, and the centre plaid exhibits a colour change.

this was done by girls working with shears. In the 1830s however a machine was introduced to do the job. The shawl was passed several times beneath a series of revolving steel blades which sheared away the loose threads. These machines came from France and their inventor, M. Vergniais, charged £300 each. However Paisley ingenuity triumphed as usual, and home-grown versions were soon available for a cost of only £40. It was said that two-thirds of the weight of yarn would be removed during the clipping process, and that this was one of the incentives towards the production of a reversible shawl. Fringing was the next operation in the finishing of the shawl. Sometimes this meant the hemming of the woven material and the sewing on of a ready-manufactured fringe. The traditional method however was for the warp ends of the shawl to be cut to the required length and then the girls in the warehouse would spit on their hands and roll small bunches of the warp

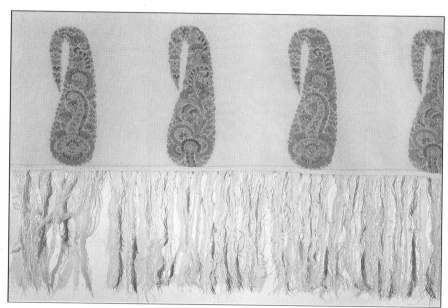

1840s woollen shawl with ready-made fringing sewn on.

1860s cotton plaid with a twisted warp fringe.

threads between their damp palms. But eventually this process was also taken over by a machine.

The final processes were the washing, stenting and calendering of the shawl. It seems that washing was necessary because of the local custom that the weavers' wives could wear the shawls in the interval between them coming off the loom and being handed over to the warehouse. Stenting was a process by which the fabric was stretched to give it elasticity and finally the steam pressing (or calendering) gave the shawl a beautiful sheen which lasted until the shawl was first washed. It is interesting to note that some of the manufacturers offered a service by which the ladies could periodically return their shawls to the warehouse to be recalendered.

The printing of pine-pattern shawls was almost a separate industry though it is known that some manufacturers produced both woven and printed shawls. We know that printed shawls of chintz were produced quite early in Scotland as an advertisement in the *Glasgow Mercury* in 1785 refers to some stolen from a printshop. Then from 1794, for four years, the Board of Manufacturers offered premiums to the best printed chintz shawls. They were eventually discontinued because they were being 'made in abundance and the manufacture quite well understood'. Three pattern books of the firm of Todd, Shortridge and Company dated 1785-1802 survive. This Dunbartonshire firm gives us our earliest evidence of the printing of pine patterns which was taking place in the mid-1790s. From the stepped outlines of these designs it is fair to

Two Paisley shawl printing blocks. The larger block is carved directly from the wood, but the smaller square block has its pattern formed by metal strips.

1840s printed shawl. Here the sprig pattern in the centre shows clearly where the edge of each printing block fell.

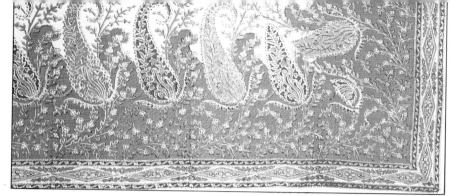

conclude that the prints are copies of woven patterns. Despite these early examples, Paisley seems to have come fairly late to the business of printing shawls. Perhaps one of the reasons why Paisley prospered was that new fields were never pioneered, leaving the town able to build upon and profit from the experience of others. The first shawls printed in Paisley were onto the fine silk gauzes that the town had been famed for in earlier years. These were expensive, high-quality articles and the standard achieved shows that the printers must have been just as highly skilled as the weavers. Patterns would be produced by the same designers who worked for the weavers, and they would be passed on to the block-cutters. The early blocks were produced wholly from the wood (usually lime), with the pattern either burnt or carved out. Later blocks had the pattern formed from fine strips of copper inserted into a hardwood base. The blocks averaged about 1 foot (0.3 m) square and different blocks which interlinked at the edges would be produced for different sections of the design. It was also necessary to produce a block for each separate colour used in each section. So if one had a shawl portraying four different design elements and five colours printed onto the plain background, then the block-cutters would need to produce twenty different blocks. All these blocks had to match-up (or 'register') exactly or the design would be spoilt by the colours blurring into one another. The actual printing process consisted of a roller for spreading the dye onto the block which the printer would then place into position on the fabric. The initial effort in producing the blocks was proportionally great, but once the blocks were ready, an infinite number of shawls in a variety of colour combinations could be produced. This naturally led to a much cheaper sale price for the printed shawls than for their woven predecessors.

Thus Paisley was involved in two diverse and profitable methods of producing shawls '. . . in imitation of the Indian' and grew to be an acknowledged world leader in the field of fancy textiles. With the end of the trade in shawls not all the expertise was lost and many of the ancillary industries such as cornflour production, dyeing and finishing remained to help keep the Paisley economy healthy. It is sad that today no remnant of that once great weaving industry remains.

The Hundred Year Fashion

The popular belief is that it was the soldiers of Napoleon Bonaparte who first brought Kashmir shawls to the notice of fashionable European ladies, having encountered them whilst on campaign in the Near East. However we know that this cannot be true, since shawls were fashionable in Britain long before Napoleon had even left his native Corsica. In fact this is one of the very few occasions when Britain can be said to be ahead of Paris in a matter of fashion!

In their native land, Kashmir shawls had been so highly prized that one prince would make a gift of a shawl to another of exalted rank. These items, naturally enough, came to the notice of officers of the British East India Company, who started to bring a few examples back as gifts for their wives or sweethearts. The unique quality of the cashmere wool was quickly appreciated. As early as 1767 the novelist, Laurence Sterne, mentions in a letter the shawls as a fashionable garment.

Unfortunately there were two barriers in the way of the fashionable woman of the 1770s who wished to own a Kashmir shawl. The first was their scarcity; each shawl took the weaver, using the traditional twill-tapestry weave, between two and three years to complete. The second was the price. Because of their comparative rarity, the mid-eighteenth century Kashmir shawls cost something in the region of 200 to 300 guineas (£210–£315). Obviously only the very richest of women could afford such luxurious garments, but nevertheless demand for them grew.

Textile manufacturers in Britain were forced to think in terms of imitating the Kashmir shawls, but the earliest attempts did not resemble

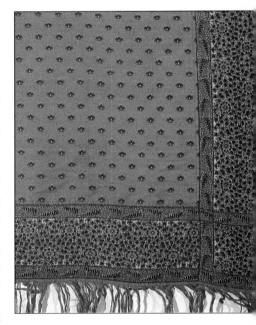

Early imitation shawl, c 1800.

Turn-over shawl c 1820, draped to show all four borders.

the originals at all closely. This was because the manufacturers here were trying to produce imitation shawls without using the laborious techniques employed in Kashmir. Manufacturers also had to contend with inferior wools. The Kashmir weavers had the monopoly of the genuine cashmere wool, so many experiments were made in Europe to try and simulate its unique softness. These were not wholly successful and the manufacturers would receive occasional complaints about the quality of their fabrics compared with those of Kashmir.

The earliest British imitations were priced at about £20 (considerably less than the Kashmir variety) and were made mainly of silk. One type was square with patterned borders sewn onto plain or sprigged centres. A variation on this idea was to sew two adjacent borders to the right side of the central area, and the other two to the wrong side. Thus when the shawl was folded diagonally all four borders could be seen to best advantage. These were known as 'turn-over' shawls. Another type had a rectangular plain centre with deep end borders of Indian design and narrower side borders (these narrow borders often were nothing more than a closely packed row of sprigs within bordering bands). Plain-centre shawls were normally made in white at first but gradually shawls appeared with centres of black, red, blue, orange and other colours. A slight change in decorative style brought in the medallion-centre shawl with infilled corners and central medallions of a floral mosaic. Amongst the weavers these were known as 'pot-lid' shawls.

Despite Britain's precedence in the shawl fashion, it was the interest of the French court, and of the Empress Josephine in particular, that finally ensured the place of the shawl in the fashionable ensemble.

Sprig-centre shawl with corner medallion, c 1810.

French fashion plate of 1823. The shawl is such a commonplace accessory that it is not even mentioned in the description.

Chenille shawl of the 1820s.

Josephine herself is said to have owned several hundred shawls and some of her portraits show them at their best. Fashions at this period were in the 'antique style' based on Greek and Roman clothing. The drape of the shawl complements this style perfectly and a well-dressed lady was then described as 'well-draped'.

The shawl entered French fashion in a really big way around 1820, not only amongst the re-emerged aristocracy but also among the middle class who aspired to their standards. The shawl became a standard part of the trousseau of the wealthy French girl, the general rule being two French shawls and one Kashmir. French taste thereafter was the dominant influence on shawl design, even reaching back to Kashmir where the native weavers were encouraged to weave to French designs.

During this early period of the shawl fashion, non-pine pattern shawls were also quite common. The damask shawl, which had a reversible pattern produced by having different coloured threads for warp and weft (often red and black), was a type originating in the Levant and much copied here. Cotton 'fur' shawls were made in imitation of shawls of real rabbit fur. Angola shawls had only a brief period of popularity, partly because their appearance was ruined by a rain shower (a distinct disadvantage in the British climate), and partly owing to their tendency to leave hairs on the arm of the wearer's escort. Chenille shawls are said to have been a Paisley invention. A Paisley manufacturer named Alexander Buchanan claimed to have produced the first chenille fabric by using a weft of a tufted cord of silk, wool or cotton. These shawls were, like the Angolas, unwashable, and therefore did not remain popular for very long.

Improvements in weaving techniques after 1820 allowed the imitation Indian patterns to become more elaborate, and to cover more of the surface of the shawl, leaving the plain centre gradually to decrease in size. Some were now woven in one piece, and in those that still had separately sewn-on borders, the borders were much wider, reaching about 12 inches (30 cm) in some cases. More coloured shawls were woven, with black and scarlet being particular favourites. The visit of George IV to Edinburgh in 1822 led to the popularisation of a new style, known at that time as the 'pale-end'. These were rectangular creamy-white centres with a border pattern of large blue pines. The 1820s also saw the first attempts to produce all-wool shawls. The Paisley firm of Robert Kerr was manufacturing these under the name of 'Thibet' shawls.

In the 1830s there was a swing away from the pine pattern towards shawls with purely naturalistic flower patterns. Manufacturers had, of course, to gamble on fashion trends, a notoriously difficult thing to do. It is said that one, when asked by his designer if he wished the pattern he was ordering to be in naturalistic style, he replied with typical Scots caution 'a wee natural, but no desperate natural!'

During the 1830s the shawl was increasingly fashionable both for indoor wear and for the carriage, and it is interesting to note that fashionable men also wore shawls. Between 1820 and 1840 a shawl was often worn over a gentleman's top coat when travelling. However, the fashion waned as the enclosed railway carriage replaced the draughty horse-drawn coach as the main mode of transport. It was also at this period that the zebra-stripe shawl was at the height of its popularity, though this was one style that the fashionable lady approved of throughout the 100-year period of the shawl.

The term shawl needs to be defined, since three distinct types each had their turn of popularity. Among the earliest was the type known as the scarf or stole shawl. These were generally more ornamental than useful and were usually about 9 feet (2.75 m) long by 20 inches (50 cm) wide. The second shape was the square shawl. The earliest examples were only about 3 feet (90 cm) square and since they were classed as handkerchiefs for export duties they became known as handkerchief shawls. Later shawls were made in any size up to 6 feet (1.85 m) square. The third shape was the long shawl which, as the name suggests, was twice as long as it was broad. These were more generally known as plaids, and commonly came in one of two sizes. Plaids were normally 10 × 5 feet (3 × 1.5 m) or even larger, and there were also three-quarter plaids which were about 8 × 4 feet (2.45 × 1.2 m). It is generally believed that whilst the shawl was worn folded diagonally with the point hanging down the wearer's back, the plaid was worn folded double and square about the shoulders. However there are few illustrations of this

Three-quarter plaid, c 1820, with particularly rich colouring.

Pale-end plaid of the 1820s.

Shawl of the 1830s with no pines in the floral pattern.

Zebra-stripe shawl, c 1840.

All-over pattern plaid, c 1860, heavy and warm enough for winter wear.

Square shawl of the mid-19th century.

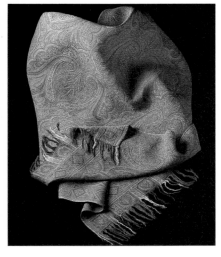

Detail from the border of an 1860s
Kirking shawl.

Kirking shawl of the 1850s.

1840s shawl which has never
undergone any clipping.

1860s reversible shawl with true
pattern on both sides.

latter method, even from the period at which the plaid was at the height of its popularity.

Fashion was of course always an influence on the shawl industry. One very striking example of this occurred in the late 1830s. An 18-year-old, fashion-conscious girl ascended the British throne in 1837 to become Queen Victoria. There was an immediate reaction in the shawl trade when it became known that she preferred the rectangular plaid to the square shawl. Very soon only a small proportion of the Paisley product was in the square form. In the 1840s fashion had another pressing reason for preferring the larger plaids with the beginnings of the crinoline era. As skirts became more voluminous, they required an adaptable over-garment. Coats to cover the crinolines were difficult to make and so the large plaids became the normal outdoor garment of the mid-nine-teenth century. By 1850 the plaid was so universally worn that its correct management indoors or out was regarded as a test of social gentility. Most moderately wealthy ladies would own at least two plaids. For the colder weather a thicker plaid which had pattern all over would be worn, and in the summer a thinner, lighter, scarlet or white centre. These white-centred plaids had developed from the earlier 'pale-ends'. They had become the universal bridal present and no lady's trousseau was complete without one. Newly-married women and young mothers almost always wore such a plaid on attending their first church service after their respective happy events. For this reason these plaids came to be known as 'Kirking shawls'.

The final development in the shawl-weaving trade in Paisley came around 1865 when a process was discovered whereby a shawl with a reversible pattern could be produced. Previous to this, because of the weaving technique, all shawls had one patterned side and one blurred unrecognisable side where all the loose threads had been shorn off. This clipping process could reduce the weight of wool in a plaid from round about 100 ounces (2800 g) of wool to between 30 (850 g) and 40 ounces (1150 g) of wool. The manufacturers naturally disliked wasting 60 to 70 oz (1700 to 2000 g) of wool on each garment and strove for many years to perfect a reversible. Unfortunately the new process trapped all the excess threads between the two patterned surfaces making the fabric much too heavy to wear if made in the large plaid size. This proved the undoing of the reversible, since Queen Victoria's lead had meant that few square shawls were being worn.

By the 1860s, mass-production techniques had led to a great drop in the price of the European imitation shawls. A table of the prices of several leading Paisley manufacturers drawn up in 1862, shows that the all-over pattern (or harness) plaids ranged from seventeen shillings and sixpence (87p) to forty-six shillings (£2.30) with an average price of twenty-seven shillings and one penny (£1.35). Whilst this was a great

Woman wearing a Scotch Plaid photographed in Paisley High Street.

saving against an original Kashmir (still selling at around £200), it represented about four weeks wages to a Paisley weaver, and therefore woven plaids were not often seen amongst the working classes.

A shawl of some kind had however become a favoured garment amongst working-class women by the middle of the century, but they tended not to be of the imitation Indian type. More often they would be large, warm, checkered garments of the type known as the Scotch Plaid. Perhaps it was this working-class interest in the shawl as a garment that stimulated the large-scale production of printed shawls in the 1850s and 1860s.

As yet no conclusive evidence has been produced as to the date of the commencement of shawl printing in Paisley, but it is likely that it was some time in the 1830s. This is strange since there is evidence that pine-patterned shawls were being printed across the Clyde in the Dumbarton area as early as the 1780s. Perhaps Paisley's manufacturers did not see as

Paisley pattern shawl c 1850, printed on to a fabric of silk gauze with satin stripes.

This printed plaid, c 1860, very closely imitates the contemporary woven examples.

much potential profit in printing as in the weaving of imitation shawls. It may have been the trade depressions of the 1820s, 1830s and 1840s which changed their minds.

It seems, however, that the earliest shawls printed in the Paisley area were not intended to be copies of the woven variety produced with the cheaper end of the market in mind. Instead, they were delicate silk gauzes intended for summer or glamorous evening wear, which would have been far above the pockets of the working classes. The manufacturers eventually did produce cheap printed imitation Indian shawls, and the 1862 list shows average prices of seven shillings and eightpence (38p) for a printed plaid and three shillings and sixpence (15p) for a printed shawl. This would be much more within the reach of a Paisley weaving family.

The beginning of the end for the shawl fashion was seen by 1865, when the crinoline skirt began to flatten at the front and bunch up at the back as a prelude to the bustle. By 1870 the bustle, with all its frills and fripperies at the rear was the mode, and soon the fashionable lady resented the way her shawl or plaid hid all the finest attributes of her latest outfit. Paisleys began to be replaced by mantles, capes and dolmans. By 1875 shawls were only to be seen on old ladies or the very poor, and even in the country villages they were regarded as old-fashioned by the 1880s. Altogether, from Sterne's letter to the coming of the bustle, the shawl in one form or another had remained a fashionable garment for a century. Knowing how quickly fashions come and go today, it is surely a tribute to the adaptability of the shawl that it was able to remain popular for so long.

The Paisley Shawl, however, did not disappear completely in the 1870s and many women still respected and treasured them. Some ladies' magazines published directions for turning a plaid or shawl into a mantle without cutting the material. In this way, should the shawl ever come back into fashion, the mantle could be unpicked and the undamaged shawl reworn. A fashion revival occurred in 1879 when for one season only the Kashmir shawl was again in vogue for outdoor wear. In 1904 it was noted that Norwegian peasant girls still wore Paisley shawls on Sundays, as did Spanish señoras. In 1908 shawls, including Paisleys, were being wound around the neck with a collarless opera cloak, or were draped classically around the shoulders. By 1917 there was a craze for turning Paisley plaids into coats, which the fashion commentator did not expect to last because of the high cost of obtaining plaids.

The town of Paisley itself, long after shawls had gone out of fashion had a high enough regard for its most famous products, to think them worthy of becoming royal gifts. In 1922 the town presented an 1834 silk white-centred three-quarter plaid to Princess Mary on the occasion of her wedding, and also a Paisley shawl was presented to Queen Elizabeth, wife of George VI, in 1938. More recently, since 1976 the world-renowned firm, Liberty's of London, has been selling a revived version of the Paisley shawl printed on to cashmere wool.

Fashion plate of 1879, when the Kashmir shawl returned to fashion for one season.

The Shawl Makers

Tradition tells us that the shawl trade was introduced to Paisley, a town with a long history of weaving, by an Edinburgh manufacturer in 1805. The story goes that he had too many orders for his own weavers to fill and, knowing that highly skilled weavers in Paisley were out of work due to a depression in the silk industry, partly caused by Napoleon's Continental Blockade, he sent work for them to try. The first contemporary reference to the shawl trade occurs in John Wilson's book written in 1812. He mentions that 'now about 100 looms (are) employed in weaving silk fabrics consisting of richly ornamented shawls and plaids . . .'. Trade Directories from Paisley help us to chart the progress of the industry. Unfortunately the early editions list all textile producers under the title of 'manufacturer', but by 1827 there are eight firms who are specialised enough to describe themselves as 'shawl manufacturer'. The Paisley manufacturers had recognised the potential of this new trade. They were known locally as 'big corks' and they were the leaders of the industry by virtue of their capital, their central premises and their organisational abilities. They bought the yarn and designs, distributed the work amongst the weavers, and sold the finished products, either from their own premises or to drapers who would then sell them to their customers. The trade quickly brought prosperity to the town. From eight in 1827, the number of manufacturers increased dramatically to a mid-1830s total of twenty-seven. The trade must have been extremely good at this time for we are also told that in 1834 shawls estimated at a value of £1,000,000 were made in the town.

For an industry which stood or fell by the standards of its operatives,

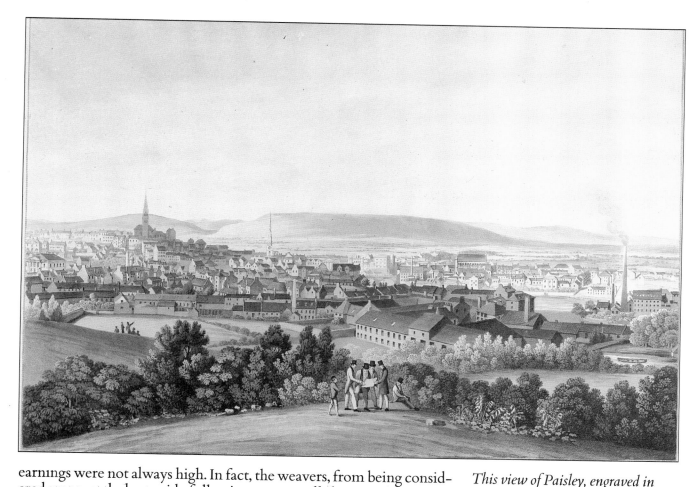

earnings were not always high. In fact, the weavers, from being considered amongst the best paid of all artisans, eventually became the weakest link in the chain of production. At the beginning of the nineteenth century a good weaver could make up to three guineas (£3.15) per week, but by the late 1830s the level of wages had fallen to about seven shillings (35p) per week. This drop can be seen as a direct consequence of the organisation of the shawl industry. In the cause of efficiency the manufacturers introduced division of labour, leaving the weaver with only the actual mechanical process of weaving the fabric. He could no longer use the inventiveness for which he had been famed, and was merely instructed to weave the patterns required.

The adoption of the Jacquard loom was yet another nail in the coffin of the so-called 'gentleman weaver'. The new looms were more expensive to buy and run than the earlier drawlooms. And, whereas most weavers with only rudimentary skill at carpentry had been capable of building their own drawlooms, they certainly did not have the technical equipment or skill required to build the Jacquard machines. The cost of

This view of Paisley, engraved in 1825, shows the town in the first flush of prosperity brought by the shawl weaving trade.

This piece of complicated machinery was beyond the technical capabilities of the home loom-builder.

These buildings in Forbes Place, Paisley, were purpose built shawl warehouses of the 1830s, from which production was co-ordinated by the manufacturers.

Kerr's shawl factory at Seedhills.

sets of pattern cards was also prohibitive to the weavers, with a set of cards for a large plaid perhaps costing over £100. As a result of the introduction of the Jacquard, many of the independent cottage workers were finally transformed into factory hands. An industrial capitalist was required who could buy and install a large number of looms under one roof. Until 1840 the premises of R. Kerr and Sons in Thread Street (one of very few early shawl factories) had employed 35 looms. When Kerr decided to turn to the Jacquard he erected a large new factory at Seedhills with 182 looms. This establishment was considered to be one of the largest and best weaving premises in Europe. However the increase in the number of looms used must have meant the employment of some 150 weavers away from their cottage loomshops, resulting naturally in a further loss of independence for the men concerned.

The shawl trade not only brought prosperity to Paisley however; in its wake followed periods of depression and slump. Many factors contributed to these depressions, but foremost amongst them was the rapid and bewildering rate of the changes in fashion. Each design would be copied by other manufacturers, leading to over-production and an inevitable fashion reaction against something considered to be getting 'common'. Meanwhile, manufacturers would have built up a large stock which they would need to clear before they could afford to commission their weavers to produce more stock. A contemporary observer noted that 'In those days the weaving trade was the staple and only industry of importance in the town with the inevitable result that, when at any time a dullness of trade came on, there was a great amount of suffering and poverty'. These periodic depressions would, in fact, bring many to the edge of starvation. Soup kitchens would be set up, and often shopkeepers went out of business because no one had any money to buy their goods.

John Henderson (1797–1851) was Provost of Paisley from 1841 to 1844, the period of the worst trade recession the town ever experienced.

The years 1841 to 1843 saw the worst slump in Paisley's history, when 67 out of 112 manufacturers went bankrupt. In February 1842, 14,791 weavers and members of their dependent families were receiving relief. This period has been described as the worst depression ever to have hit a British city. The Provost, John Henderson, stated that people coming to him to ask for relief had often had to borrow items of clothing from neighbours because they had sold their own to buy food. In fact the Government were so worried about the potentially explosive situation at Paisley, that the Prime Minister and Home Secretary of the time began an undercover scheme, run by a civil servant named Edward Twistleton, to help provide some relief for the townsfolk. For a Government which believed in 'laissez-faire', this was an admission that things were very bad in the town. It is estimated that in 1841 more than £50,000 was distributed to the stricken in the form of food and clothing. The town of Paisley itself went bankrupt in 1842, and was not in a position to repay its debts for some thirty years.

In an effort to alleviate the suffering, Queen Victoria lent her support. Not only did she make a nationwide appeal for funds, but in 1842 she purchased seventeen shawls, and as a mark of her sympathy for Paisley, she is reputed to have worn one to the baptism of the Prince of Wales (the future King Edward VII). Thirty specimen shawls, with a total retail value of £157 5s 6d (£157.27), had been sent to her on approval. From them she chose one or more shawls from the work of each manufacturer represented. She paid a total of £91 for her seventeen shawls, though not all of these were 'Paisley' pattern, as tartan and velvet

This illustration from the catalogue of the 1851 Crystal Palace Exhibition typifies the trend at that time for blending the purely abstract form of the pine with much more realistic flowers and foliage.

Three typical Paisley weavers, Messrs Ritchie, Kilpatrick and Cornell.

shawls were also included. After this gesture many orders for shawls were placed and the trade began to enjoy a revival. Another great boost to the Paisley trade was the appearance of the shawl at the Trade Exhibitions in 1851 and 1862 where the official reports made special mention of the excellence of the product.

The Paisley weavers themselves, at least during the early years of the nineteenth century, were renowned throughout Scotland for their intellectual capacity. Their development in this direction was favoured by their occupation. It was a quiet job and also one that could be left for a period of time without spoiling, and therefore the weavers had the opportunity to think and to discuss the burning subjects of the day. Another advantage was that the weaving was done in a loomshop of four or six looms and they could therefore hold discussions and debates as they worked. This is emphasised by their attitude to technical developments. If one of them thought up a good improvement for his loom, he would share it around, and the constructive criticism of his workmates would help to bring the idea to fruition. This was naturally good for Paisley's trade in general. The weavers were also political animals, following the Radical cause with enthusiasm. Each loomshop would combine to buy a weekly newspaper so that they could keep up with events. Many of the weavers were Chartists and momentous meetings were held in the town where Patrick Brewster, a minister of Paisley Abbey and leader of Scotland's 'moral-force' Chartists, argued fiercely that peaceful protest achieved more than the violent outbursts encouraged by Feargus O'Connor (leader of the 'physical-force' Chartists). In religion the weavers traditionally belonged to the various dissenting churches, and today Paisley has a rich heritage of non-conformist congregations, with Methodists, Baptists, Congregationalists, Pentecostalists, Mormons and even Spiritualists active in the town. If a group of weavers in Paisley decided that none of the churches in the town had ideas matching theirs, then they were quite willing to set up on their own! One such instance occurred in the late 1790s when a group broke away from the Baptists and ran a flourishing congregation for some thirty years.

A vital part of the weaving community during the early years of the century was the drawboy. He was the weaver's assistant who was necessary in the working of the loom. In some contemporary accounts it has been claimed that the drawboys were nothing better than rogues and rapscallions, terrorising the neighbourhood in roving gangs whenever they were not working. However, newspaper articles written by former drawboys, which appeared in 1904 shortly after the publication of Matthew Blair's book on the shawl trade, denied these allegations. They pointed out that drawboys were not the lowest of the low socially and they came from a broad spectrum of Paisley life, from the manufac-

Front page of one of the papers read by the Paisley Weavers, which includes two job adverts in connection with the shawl industry.

Statue of the Reverend Patrick Brewster erected by the people of Paisley in 1863.

This was the West Relief Church erected in Paisley in 1781 for those who had split away from the established church. It was well attended by the weaving fraternity.

The Paisley Advertiser.

Vol. VII. No. 727.　　　SATURDAY MORNING, SEPTEMBER 8, 1838.　　　Price Fourpence Halfpenny.

turers' sons to the poor orphans. They were, in fact, skilled workers and were probably the highest paid working boys in the town, taking home an average of three shillings and sixpence (17p) to help keep their families. That they worked hard and for long hours is certain, so perhaps they should have been forgiven some show of exuberance during their non-working hours.

Descriptions of the weaving shops allow us to form a fairly clear picture of the working conditions of the weavers. The three main weaving areas in the town were the central area around George Street and Canal Street, the West End particularly Broomlands Street, Ferguslie and West Campbell Street, and, what was then virtually a separate village to the south of Paisley, Charleston. Most houses at that period were either one or two storeys high, three-storey tenements being rare and four storeys unknown. The loomshop would be on the ground floors of the buildings, and the floors would be earthen (the fact that the rarely cleared refuse middens were close to the back doors, and drainage was primitive or non-existent must have meant that the interiors were somewhat insanitary). There would be windows to both back and front of the building and a fireplace opposite the door. The earth floor would generally be 12 to 18 inches (30 to 45 cm) lower than the doorstep to give the extra roof height required by the looms, and beneath each loom a further pit would be excavated to accommodate the treadles. Most of the weavers lived in rooms above the loomshops, or, in the older cottages, the loomshop would be at one side of the close and the weaver's home, usually one room and kitchen, at the other. In this home the weaver's wife had to work equally as hard as her husband. Alongside the housework and the childminding, she was usually given the job of pirn-winding. This was the winding of the weft yarns onto the pirns which fitted into the shuttles. Consequently every house would have its pirn-wheel in the corner.

In the loomshop itself there would be four or six looms according to the floor space and each loom would be placed next to a window to make the best possible use of the natural light. In addition, gas lighting began to be installed in the loomshops from 1823. In the 1830s the gas company fixed special rates for the weavers. For eight shillings (40p), payable in advance, they could use the gas from 7 a.m. to sunrise, and from sunset to 10 p.m. between 15th September and 1st April, (which gives a fair idea of what were considered to be normal working hours). Fire was a hazard, particularly when the gas lights were on. It took only one harness thread to snap and fall over the open gas jet to set the whole harness and web alight in seconds. However, the dreary working surroundings were often alleviated by visitors to the shops, such as weavers who were waiting for a new web to be set onto their looms, or the waste gatherers. These were men who would gather every waste scrap of

This typical late 18th century weaving cottage (now demolished) was the birthplace of Robert Tannahill in 1774.

Early interior photograph of the weaving shop at 37 George Street, Paisley.

This old lady was photographed at her pirn wheel in South Campbell Street in Paisley.

thread in the shop for which they would 'pay' the weavers a few matches. Later, when they had gathered enough waste, they would sort it into wool and cotton and resell it. They were always welcome in the loom-shops because they also gathered the whole town's gossip in the course of their journeyings. Children were also frequent visitors to the loom-shops where they could perhaps get paste to aid their kite making, or they might be given broken shuttles, the metal points of which could be turned into spinning tops.

Naturally a weaver's life was not all work. In common with all Scots they vigorously celebrated the coming of the New Year, when the normal everyday diet of porridge, potatoes and vegetables would be supplemented by an abundance of cheese, heaps of oatmeal cakes seasoned with carvie seeds, perhaps a joint of beef from the cow (which many weaving families would buy in spring, fatten and then slaughter in autumn), and of course a bottle or two of the hard stuff! It was a season of universal hospitality, mirth and madness. Another annual holiday was known as Sma Shot Day. The Sma Shot was a binding thread woven into the cloth for strength. It was vital but, because it was not actually seen on the surface, the manufacturers refused to pay for the yarn used on it. After protracted disputes the manufacturers eventually capitulated, and the Sma Shot Day holiday was instituted in 1856 in celebration. It became the custom for weavers to march in procession carrying their banners to the river pier and then to spend the day in a steamboat trip down the Clyde. As well as such holidays as these, the weavers enjoyed a reasonable amount of leisure time. In good weather they would often gather at the close-mouths during mealtimes to enjoy a chat and a smoke. Similarly, during the season when the gas lighting was not in use in the loomshops, work would stop at the gloamin and again the weavers would gather to discuss or tell stories until dark. Generally speaking the weaver was his own master as far as timekeeping was concerned, since he was paid by the piece and not by the hour. He could stop work and go for a walk if he so desired. As a result there grew among the weavers a great appreciation of the beauty of the countryside around Paisley. A tradition developed amongst the gentlemen weavers for versifying, and Paisley produced a whole string of minor poets, the most celebrated being Robert Tannahill. The weavers were also noted for their interest in the natural sciences. Many were bird-fanciers and kept caged canaries in their loomshops. An equal number were keen horticulturalists, and there must have been many fine gardens in the area. Paisley in fact boasts the oldest horticultural society in Scotland, founded in 1782. Gardeners in Paisley were particularly noted for their cultivation of the laced pink, of which they are said to have bred 150 different varieties. The main

Robert Tannahill (1774-1810), Paisley's best known weaver-poet. The portrait may not be a true likeness since it was painted posthumously.

Medal awarded in 1860, after a curling match between two of the four large Paisley clubs.

DOUBLE CLOTH TABLE OF PRICES

PER 5000 SHOTS,

AGREED TO BY MANUFACTURERS AND WEAVERS OF PAISLEY,

1st FEBRUARY, 1866. TYE 320.

Splits Warp in 2 Yds. Wide.	SPLIT HARNESS Tweeled with Two or Four Leaves.	
2400	1200	1s 11d
2600	1300	1s 11d
2800	1400	1s 11½d
3000	1500	2s
3200	1600	2s 0½d
3400	1700	2s 1d
3600	1800	2s 1½d
3800	1900	2s 2d
4000	2000	2s 2½d
4200	2100	2s 3d
4400	2200	2s 3½d
4600	2300	2s 4d
4800	2400	2s 4½d

Splits Warp in 2 Yds. Wide.	THREAD HARNESS.	
2400	1200	1s 11½d
2600	1300	1s 11½d
2800	1400	2s 0¼d
3000	1500	2s 1d
3200	1600	2s 1¾d
3400	1700	2s 2½d
3600	1800	2s 3¼d
3800	1900	2s 4d
4000	2000	2s 4¾d
4200	2100	2s 5½d
4400	2200	2s 6¼d
4600	2300	2s 7d
4800	2400	2s 7¾d

Splits Warp in 2 Yds. Wide.	½ Split & ½ Thread Harness, Tweeled with 6 Leaves, or Split Harness with 8 Leaves.	
2400	1200	2s 1d
2600	1300	2s 1d
2800	1400	2s 1¾d
3000	1500	2s 2½d
3200	1600	2s 3¼d
3400	1700	2s 4d
3600	1800	2s 4¾d
3800	1900	2s 5½d
4000	2000	2s 6¼d
4200	2100	2s 7d
4400	2200	2s 7¾d
4600	2300	2s 8½d
4800	2400	2s 9¼d
5000	2500	2s 10d
5200	2600	2s 10¾
5400	2700	2s 11½d
5600	2800	3s 0¼d
5800	2900	3s 1d
6000	3000	3s 1¾d
6200	3100	3s 2½d
6400	3200	3s 3¼d
6600	3300	3s 4d
6800	3400	3s 4¾d
7000	3500	3s 5½d
7200	3600	3s 6¼d
7400	3700	3s 7d

EXTRAS for Undernoted Tyes.	
380	0½d
440	1d
500	1½d
560	2d
640	2½d
720	3d
800	3½d
880	4d
960	4½d
1060	5d
1160	5½
1260	6d
1360	6½d
1460	7d
1560	7½d
1660	8d
1760	8½d
1860	9d

NOTE 1. Warps two yards in width, with less than 2400 Splits, to be paid as 2400 Splits.
" 2. Warps over two yards in width to be paid ½d. per 50 Splits extra.
" 3. Warps under two yards in width to be paid ¼d. per 50 Splits less.
" 4 The above two yards understood to be exclusive of Selvages.
" 5. Cashmere warps or "All Silk," in warps and weft, to be paid 2d extra.
" 6. Two-fold Woollen yarn, under 1800 warps, to be paid same as Cashmere ; at and above 1800 warps, to be paid 1d. more.

G. CALDWELL & Co. PRINTERS.

An example of a weavers' price table.

active sport to have attracted the weavers was curling, though the somewhat similar summer sports of bowling and quoits were also patronised. During spells of suitable winter weather, work might stop for days on end whilst the curling passion was indulged.

Saturday was pay day for the weavers when any finished fabric would be taken to the warehouse for inspection. Great queues often developed in the face of this lengthy task, so the wise weaver would send a member of his family to hold his place in the queue whilst he had a leisurely shave and dressed in decent clothes. Afterwards, being pay day, the Saturday meal would always be a good one, with the afternoon and evening free for pursuing leisure activities. A favourite summer excursion was for the whole family to walk the three miles to Renfrew, and there have a picnic on the banks of the River Clyde, watching the many steamers pass. A number of weavers might pass their Saturday afternoons fishing in the Black Cart Water for eels, perch, flounders and sometime pike and trout, which would of course provide a welcome addition to the family's supper menu. On Sunday mornings they would rise early and take a stroll before breakfast but often that was the only recreation they allowed themselves on the Sabbath. Most of the weavers were church-going men and some were particularly strict about Sabbath observation, not even allowing their children to play or laugh out loud. On Sunday evenings it was customary for the whole household to gather together for family prayers before retiring to bed early to prepare for the beginning of another week's labour.

In the face of a threat to their livelihood, the evening discussions of the weavers would take on a more serious aspect. There was a strong trade union which kept a close eye on such matters as the fixed-price tables, which were agreements between the Union and the manufacturers as to the price to be paid for every different type of weaving in Paisley. Because of the keenness of competition, the manufacturers often asked the weavers to take a reduction in rates. This was always referred to the Union which might refuse if trade was good, but if it was bad they would sometimes agree to a temporary reduction. Unscrupulous manufacturers might take advantage of this by increasing production, stockpiling finished goods until trade improved and they could be sold for a higher rate. For the upkeep of a Union to combat such moves each weaver paid a quarterly sum to his district branch. These branches, each of which was entitled to send delegates to the central committee, were the major constituents of the Paisley Weavers' Union. Each branch had its own symbol. The Charleston branch proudly bore a drum which was said to have been carried at the Battle of Waterloo. When a branch meeting was called the drum was paraded through the streets and beaten, a small act of defiance on the part of the weavers since, by an ancient (and largely disregarded) law, it was illegal to call a meeting 'by tuck of drum'. If a district meeting was unable to resolve a particular problem then a general meeting would be called, and these were often very stormy indeed. The Union operated a system of fining and/or expelling any member who did not co-operate in an agreed boycotting of a manufacturer. If a manufacturer proved to be particularly recalcitrant in his dealings with the Union, then it was not unknown for his effigy to be paraded through the streets of the town before being ceremoniously burnt. The following poem, written by one of Paisley's minor poets, describes one such incident, as well as epitomising Paisley, the weaving town, during the first half of the nineteenth century.

The drum beaten through the streets to call the Charleston District weavers to a meeting.

The Dooslan Stane, standing at the corner of Rowan Street and Neilston Road, was one of the main rallying points of the Charleston weavers.

When I was a Drawboy
BY DUNCAN McFARLANE McNEIL 1889

In the village o' Charleston, near Paisley toun,
I there was brocht up mony years noo gane roun',
When plides were in vogue, an' the weavin' was thrang,
And the swing o' the 'lay' was aye heard wi' a bang.
The click o' the shuttle, an' whirr o' the wheel,
The tramp o' the treadles, an' swish o' the 'deil',
The shout tae 'draw't up', or the notes o' a sang,
Were heard a' aroun' as ye steppt alang —
When I was a drawboy.

Some guid folk were in it, an' that is quite true;
Some bien folk were in it, but o' them mighty few;
But they a' had the knack baith to speak an' discuss —
'Bout religion and politics they made a big fuss.
At Union Street corner, what disputes took place!
Till some wid turn red an' some white in the face,
I've thocht aft sin' syne, an' it isna a joke,
That they were funny bodies, the Charleston folk —
When I was a drawboy.

On Mondays in thae days the looms made nae din,
For the 'lay' was at rest wi' the hard 'pookin' pin';
They were a' their ain masters — they hadna a boss —
Some played at the bullets, some played pitch-an'-toss.
Nae police tae fash them or roar in their lugs,
Some had great cock-battles, an' some foucht their dogs;
An whiles at the en' o't, the truth for tae tell,
The principals aft had a battle themsel —
When I was a drawboy.

What a noise an' rinnin', and o' what dispute,
When a meetin' was ca'd, and the drum was sent oot!
When a Causeyside magnate wid prices reduce
There was rinnin', an' stumpin', an' muckle abuse;
An' his effigy hung up 'tween twa mid-room lums,
Wi' its belly filled fu' o' tar'd ravelins an' thrums —
What shots they fir'd intil't till late in the nicht,
An' then it illumed the hale street wi' its licht —
When I was a drawboy.

But that has a' gane noo for mony a year,
And the click o' the shuttle you'll scarcely noo hear;
The 'tail' and the 'simple' the 'lashes' and a',
Wi' the 'deil' and the drawboy, hae pass'd clean awa',
And the place noo looks better than what it did then;
And may it be better in women and men,
And healthier, and cleaner, and happier too,
Then when the first 'lash' and first 'simple' I drew —
When I was a drawboy.

Eventually as the shawl went out of fashion trade declined. It is possible that depressions in the luxury shawl trade had tempted manufacturers to stimulate demand lower down the scale by producing cheaper qualities. This unfortunately had the effect of driving out of fashion the high-class article without which the trade simply could not survive. By this time most of the weavers were old men. The younger weavers had seen that there could be no future for a weaving industry equipped solely with handlooms unable to compete with the powerlooms of other weaving centres. Fortunately the end of the shawl fashion co-incided with the great build-up of the heavy engineering industries of Clydeside, providing an alternative source of employment for the younger men. Not everyone foresaw the inevitable. Writing in 1872, William Cross talks of the shawl trade 'which, I am glad to hear, is now sounder than ever, though much curtailed in extent'. Obviously he saw the decline as nothing worse than yet another of the periodic depressions the trade suffered. However a few years later the local paper in response to a suggestion that it would be good to see the shawl trade thriving once more, declared that Paisley should not again become a town dependent on the female whim. It went on to state 'fashion is too fickle a structure on which to rest . . . Of this Paisley has had experience in the past, and we are sure she does not wish it repeated'.

With the decline, the remaining weavers had to find whatever substitute weaving work they could. Distress was widespread, particularly amongst those weavers who still owned their own looms rather than renting from a manufacturer. Some manufacturers managed to turn to other textiles for, with the disruption of France and Prussia resulting from their 1870 war, there was an upswing in Britain's textile industry as a whole. Again however, it was work for powerlooms, and it was only the fact that cheaper shawl fabrics had always been produced that saved the handloom industry from total extinction in 1870. The looms now turned to the manufacture of such items as tartan or rep shawls, and ponchos which are said to have been exported to South America (a clear case of coals to Newcastle). As a result of the easy adaptability of the Jacquard looms to this work, it was even considered that Paisley might again become an important textile centre. Other products of the period included tapestry curtains, table covers, bedcovers, petticoats and

Tartan shawl of the 1870s, made by Daniel Murray Junior & Co., Paisley.

20th century fur shawl made on the loom in Paisley Museum.

butchers' aprons. There was also a small but steady trade in what were known as 'velvet' or 'fur' shawls. One or two enterprising firms took over old premises on Causeyside and fitted them up with old discarded looms. One firm installed sixty looms, twenty of which were actually brought into the town from Alva near Stirling, along with the weavers who had previously worked them. This factory employed about forty weavers producing fur and velvet shawls, many of which were exported to southern and western Ireland. The hopes of an upswing in trade were not to be realised, but because of the steady work it was not until 1890 that the number of manufacturers fell below ten. The last harness shawl ever woven in Paisley was made by Messrs. Waters and Cook of Thread Street on 12th June 1903. The firm had received an order for a few shawls, so they ran off one web. It was only during the Second World War, however, that the last firm weaving fur shawls on handlooms, Heiton, Clark and Company, finally closed down.

So Paisley's gradual move towards single-minded concentration on the fancy shawl trade had served the town ill in the end. When the shawl was no longer fashionable weaving died out, and only the more adaptable ancillary industries such as thread, starch and dyeing have survived to the present day.

Paisley's Competitors

It must always be remembered that not all shawls made '. . . in imitation of the Indian' came from Paisley, although the name of the town was attached (by English speakers) to the shawl as a descriptive term. Similarly, in France, all the 'pine' patterned shawls are termed 'cachemire' regardless of their Oriental or European origins. The British may have been first in the field of imitating the Kashmir shawls, but they were by no means the only ones to do so. And there were always genuine Kashmir shawls to be had.

Shawls had been woven by the laborious twill-tapestry technique in Kashmir since the fifteenth century, acquiring the būtā design some hundred years before the first shawls found their way to Europe. By 1800 the export trade was well established and many merchants maintained agents in the Kashmir capital Srinagar. According to William Moorcroft, by 1822 the Kashmiris were already very adept at suiting their various different shawl types to the tastes of the markets they were intended for.

By the middle of the century the merchants had become very prosperous through catering for the increasingly dominant foreign taste. Around 1850 it is known that French agents had begun to attempt to 'improve' the native product by taking to Kashmir, designs formulated in Paris. Soon Kashmir shawls entered in International Exhibitions were giving full design credit to the European agent who had commissioned them. In the decade up to 1860 shawl exports to Europe more than doubled, but after 1860 the market rapidly contracted. The Kashmir shawls were now thought to be inferior to the European examples and

Late 18th century Kashmir shawl with striped pattern.

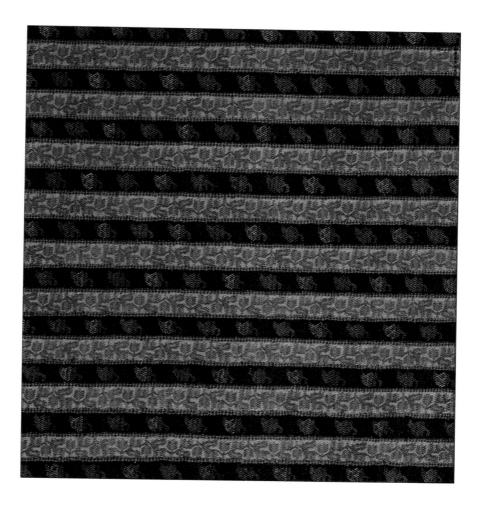

yet were still more costly to purchase. The end of the Kashmir twill-tapestry shawl industry came with the abrupt change of European fashion around 1870, although shawls embroidered onto pashmina continued to be made.

One of the hardest jobs facing any textile historian is to determine the origin of one of the European 'pine' pattern shawls. Designers were often freelance, selling their patterns to any willing buyer. For example, French-stamped designs were certainly in the hands of Paisley manufacturers. In addition manufacturers imitated each other's products and often no records survive in the various centres of production. This is particularly true of the French shawl industry.

France, where the shawl fashion took hold in the early years of the nineteenth century, was as much affected by the Continental Blockade as Paisley had been. No more genuine Kashmir shawls were being imported, leaving French manufacturers to take up the challenge of

Kashmir shawl of the 1850s.

*This design was drawn up in Paris,
but was bought for use by a Paisley
manufacturer.*

French manufacturer's label, on the reverse of an 1860s plaid with a small plain black centre.

weaving imitations. Most of the extant information on these manufacturers is in the form of entries in exhibition catalogues. Perhaps the best known name was that of Guillaume Ternaux of Reims and Paris who, for the quality of his work, was awarded the Legion of Honour by Napoleon. He was also one of many French manufacturers to experiment with producing shawls by the Kashmir twill-tapestry technique. Such shawls always proved uncommercial and so the experiments never came to fruition. It is possible therefore, though extremely rare, to find European-made shawls done in the Indian fashion.

Many of the French shawls were made of the actual cashmere goats' wool rather than the more ordinary fibres used in Britain, and this may prove to be an identifying factor. French shawls can also sometimes be identified by means of initials or the name of the manufacturers woven into the corner. However this technique is known to occur also in Paisley-made shawls. More common in France was the attaching of a label to the reverse of the shawl, usually extolling medal wins at various inter-

The name of the Paisley manufacturers, D. Spiers & Co., has been woven into the corner of this plaid.

national exhibitions. This labelling was most probably a response to competition from foreign manufacturers.

In the early years of the French shawl industry it was Paris that had the lion's share of the production, but after about 1830 Lyons took the lead with, by 1860, nearly six times as many looms as the capital. The Paris industry consequently died away with the fashion in 1870, whilst production slowed down gradually, only ending at the turn of the century, in the provinces.

Another flourishing industry was established in Vienna in the early nineteenth century. More fortunate than French historians, those who wish to study the Viennese production can turn to a collection of sample cards, founded by the Emperor Francis I in 1807. This contains some sixty documented examples of Viennese products. In addition Vienna Museum of Applied Art has shawl samples and a few complete shawls.

The shawl industry in Vienna closely parallels the British with early examples having separately sewn on borders and appliqué motifs. But by the 1820s the designs were being woven into the shawls rather than applied. In materials too there were parallels. Vienna considered its shawls of the 1820s to be products of the silk industry, but in the national industrial exhibitions of 1835, 1839 and 1845 they were classified as wool products. An 1845 shawl by Joseph Burde & Son was mentioned particularly for being completely of wool, and for causing a sensation even amongst visiting French manufacturers. However it seems it was more usual for the Viennese shawls to have a silk warp with a wool or cotton weft.

The Viennese shawl industry was set up to satisfy the demand for imitation Indian shawls in Austria. It was considered very important to beat off British and French competition within the Austrian Empire. Eventually however, a surplus was produced which went for export, the main markets being Germany, Italy, Turkey, Russia, Poland and North America. By the 1830s over 4,000 looms were at work on shawl production and by 1845 the Viennese considered their products to be competitive with the shawls from Paris and Lyons. The annual production was recorded at 400,000 shawls, of which more than two-thirds were exported.

Edinburgh and Norwich, both in the shawl business for about twenty-five years before Paisley, were the latter's main British rivals during the nineteenth century, though there were some smaller centres of production such as Stockport. The earliest years of shawl production in Britain are poorly documented but it seems that Edinburgh may have been the first centre. The records of the Board of Manufacturers tell us that a

Design registered at the Patent Office by David Sime, one of the last of the Edinburgh manufacturers.

William Mortimer was making shawls in Edinburgh as early as 1777. The Board evidently thought his work worthy of encouragement and in 1781 they awarded him a premium of £10. Other manufacturers soon became interested in this new product and by 1791 one, George Richmond, had thirteen looms working on shawls. By 1798 the Board was offering premiums for 'cheap shawls, such as servants wear', an indication that the shawl as a garment was universally popular in Scotland. By about 1810 the manufacturers were beginning to establish warehouses close to the heart of the city for better promotion of their goods. During the next twenty or so years Edinburgh reached the height of its endeavours in the shawl trade, and this was the period of growth also for its best-known firm, Gibb and MacDonald. In 1830 they were producing red, white and black shawls, which were sold to retailers for between £6 and £16. After the 1830s, however, instead of moving into the mass market as the Paisley industry did, the Edinburgh trade was concentrated in the hands of a few specialists who found the competition too much for them. The last Edinburgh shawl manufacturer seems to have been David Sime, samples of whose work are registered at the Patent Office from 1843 to 1847. He appears to have gone out of business in 1853.

It has always been particularly difficult for costume historians to identify shawls as having originated in Edinburgh for, apart from the Sime designs at the Patent Office, and a small collection of designs on oil paper stamped by the Board of Manufacturers and kept in the Library of the Edinburgh College of Art, there were no fully documented examples of Edinburgh shawls known to exist. That situation changed in 1973 when a descendant of the MacDonald of Gibb and MacDonald approached the National Museum of Antiquities of Scotland (now the Royal Museum of Scotland). She had a collection of five shawls, thirty-seven border samples, seven deep end-borders and five designs of medallion centres and corners. One group of border pieces were made wholly of silk in pale colours and were probably for 'turn-over' style shawls. Others were mixtures of silk, cotton and wool and seem to exhibit the 1830s fashion for bright patterns on dark backgrounds. The medallions seem to be intended for appliqué onto plain fabrics, and it has been speculated that this may prove to be a distinguishing feature of the Edinburgh product. The five complete shawls, though ranging in date from approximately 1805 to 1835, showed some similarities. They all had cream coloured grounds and patterns in colours which seemed subdued when compared to shawls of Paisley manufacture. A further possible distinguishing feature of the Edinburgh shawls emerged. A stripe of black in the border was found in one of the Gibb and MacDonald shawls. The same feature was also present in a shawl which Dorothy Whyte had bought because it answered closely a near contemporary description of Edinburgh shawls of 1833. It may well be that we can state with some confidence that other shawls displaying this feature are also from Edinburgh.

In Norwich the firm of Barrow and Watson were making 'shawls' as early as 1784 though it appears that these early examples were more like neckerchiefs than shawls, and were mainly made for export to America. At the same time, one John Harvey of Norwich, was mixing Norfolk yarns with Spanish, and wool with silk in an experiment to simulate the softness of the true cashmere wool. In this early period there was much

This 1830s shawl, from the Paisley Museum collection, exhibits the black stripes at the border which may be indicative of Edinburgh manufacture.

of this experimentation with yarns in Norwich, with the result that no two early shawls from the city feel alike. Another eighteenth century Norwich manufacturer, P.J. Knights, produced a 'shawl counterpane', an example of which was presented to Queen Charlotte in 1792. But in all these early Norwich products the design was darned in by girl embroideresses, rather than woven. It was around the turn of the century that the Norwich weavers discovered that they could produce a woven pattern on the drawloom. This made the damask technique used in Edinburgh until that time hopelessly expensive, and so they too had to switch to the harness. These early 'fill-overs', as they were called, seem to have taken about three weeks to weave and sold for about £40-£50. As in the other centres trade increased during the first decade of the nineteenth century, which came as a welcome relief to the Norwich manufacturers who were finding that the market for some of their traditional products was shrinking rapidly. It has been claimed that the Norwich patterns never followed the Indian originals as slavishly as did the Paisley examples. This is a surprising statement in light of the continual claims from the Norwich manufacturers that Paisley companies were copying 'our shawls not less than four out of every six we bring out'.

As in Paisley, the Jacquard loom seems to have been introduced in large numbers during the 1830s, allowing an increase both in the sophistication of the product and in the quantity produced. The order book of one firm, E. & F. Hinde, shows that in 1847-8 they sold 32,000 shawls, 4,310 of them going to a single buyer. Production was probably at its peak in the 1850s and Norwich firms received much favourable comment on the quality of their product at the 1851 Great Exhibition. In the 1860s and 1870s the most famed Norwich firm was Clabburn, Sons and Crisp, who made plaid-size shawls entirely of silk, often with a deep crimson warp. A shawl by this firm in the colours of the Danish royal family was presented to Princess Alexandra on her marriage to the Prince of Wales in 1863. However, as in Paisley, the heyday of the shawl was over in Norwich by the mid 1870s, though two small firms continued to produce shawls until their respective closures in the 1930s and 1954.

So why, in the face of such strong competition from these rival manufacturing centres, did Paisley, a comparative latecomer, reign supreme at least in Britain? The signs were there from the very start, since the answer lies both in the superior powers of organisation exhibited by the Paisley manufacturers, and in the loyalty of the workforce. Edinburgh manufacturers had to ask Paisley weavers to help fill their orders, so they cannot have been as well organised as they might have been. But the Paisley 'corks' soon picked the trade up and within only a few short years had turned Paisley into a virtual one-industry town.

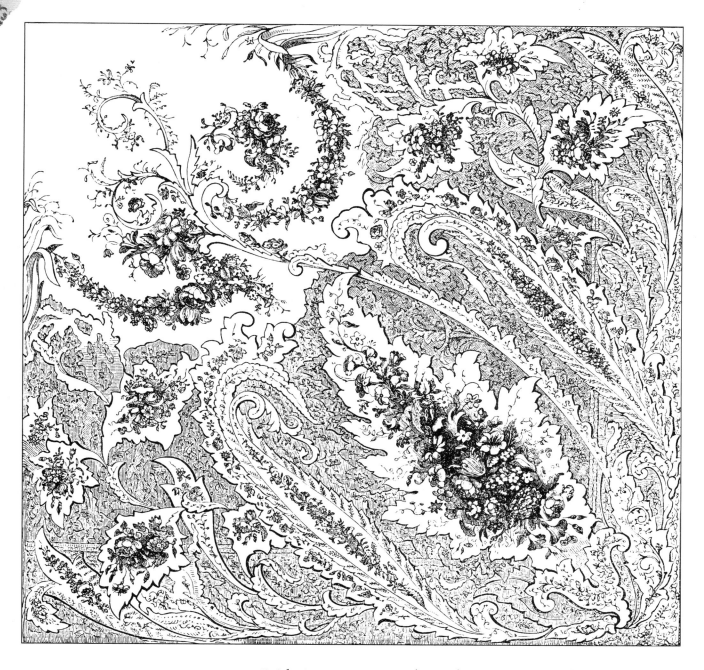

Norwich shawl illustrated in the catalogue of the Great Exhibition, 1851.

Paisley's supremacy in the trade was not immediately obvious of course. In fact shawls with the 'pine' pattern were known only as 'Imitation Indian' until well into the middle of the century. Today, most of the English-speaking world knows of the Paisley pattern and the shawls it adorned. In other parts of Europe, however, imitation Indian shawls

were always known as French, and Paisley never really managed to compete on equal terms with the French industry. Paisley manufacturers at first refused to exhibit at Crystal Palace in 1851 when they were told that they would not be able to display their prices, because they knew that their shawls could only bear comparison with the French product in terms of price.

Paisley was much more successful competing against the other British centres. The loyal workforce may well have been somewhat underpaid by manufacturers anxious to increase profits. But costs were cut in other ways too, particularly by the pirating of designs. Not having to pay their own designers gave many Paisley manufacturers an edge, allowing them, as the Norwich trade complained, to sell their goods '. . . at prices which take away our profit'. But above all Paisley went into mass production, with the eventual result that the markets of its competitors dwindled. By the 1850s the majority of shawls available in any draper's shop would have been made in Paisley. A lady wishing to purchase such a shawl would be likely to ask to see a selection of 'Paisleys'. In the course of time the name became attached to the fashion, and when the fashion ended it was transferred to the distinctive pattern, firmly putting a small Scottish manufacturing town on the world map.

All-silk plaid, similar to those woven by Clabburn, Sons & Crisp in Norwich in the 1860s.

The Paisley Museum Shawl Collection

The year 1871 saw the opening in Paisley of Scotland's first municipally-run Museum, funded by money gifted to the town's people by Sir Peter Coats, senior partner in the giant thread firm of J. & P. Coats. It was a mere coincidence that this occurred at the time of the rapid decline of Paisley's best known industry. Sad to say this great opportunity seems not to have been grasped. As far as can be gathered from the pre-1900 records of the Museum, no more than thirty shawls had been collected by the turn of the century, along with two model looms and a handful of small items of weaving equipment.

Today there are over 800 shawls in the collection backed up by other items such as the correspondence of one of the important manufacturers, many of the pattern and sample books kept by the shawl firms, data on the union organisation of the weavers, and last but not least a comprehensive selection of weaving equipment including a full-size Jacquard loom.

The impetus towards the building up of this collection came in 1902 when the Incorporated Weaving, Dyeing and Printing College of Glasgow held a special loan exhibition of 'Paisley Shawls and similar fabrics', at their halls in Calton, Glasgow. The event was reported at length in the *Paisley and Renfrewshire Gazette,* but a few weeks later the same newspaper was recording its dismay that so few Paisley Buddies had made the effort to visit the exhibition. It was therefore suggested that Paisley should stage a similar event to foster local pride.

Matthew Blair, one-time Paisley drawboy, who was in 1901 a member of the Board of Governors of the College, then wrote to the *Gazette*

Sir Peter Coats, who provided most of the money for the establishment of the Paisley Free Library and Museum.

A contemporary print view of the front elevation of Paisley Museum at the time of opening in 1871.

to propose that, rather than holding another exhibition, it would be better to concentrate on establishing a permanent and representative collection of shawls at the Museum. In the event both ideas came to fruition. In 1905 the Paisley Loan Exhibition was held, at which over 650 shawls and related exhibits were on view. Items for the exhibition were brought from as far away as London, and over 200 lenders were involved. When the exhibition closed, over twenty of these shawls were immediately donated to the Museum by their owners, and over the following six or seven years another fifteen found their way back into the collection. By the beginning of the First World War these shawls, together with other donations of that period, had formed the nucleus of a representative collection, with at least one example of most of the different types of shawl.

The war naturally slowed down the building of the collection and it was not really until the mid-1920s that it began to pick up again. The flow of shawls into the Museum was fairly steady during the 1930s, but it again suffered a blow in the early years of the Second World War.

Overleaf –

This plaid was one of four (two Kashmir and two Paisley) lent to the 1905 Exhibition by Mrs Polson (of Brown & Polson). It was donated to the Museum some two years later.

However it was the early 1940s that brought two very important dona-tions to the Museum.

In 1941 a plainloom of the type in use from the eighteenth century onwards was donated by a Kilbarchan man. But even more important was the fact that in 1943 Paisley's last remaining weaving shop closed down, and one of its two Jacquard looms was brought to the Museum. This is the loom that today forms the centre-piece of the gallery display-ing the Paisley Shawl industry.

As the 1950s and the 1960s progressed more people began donating shawls to the Museum. It was now about a hundred years since the end of the industry and more people were recognising the historical value of the shawls. This was amply demonstrated in 1964 by the biggest ever

Viewing one section of the 1905 Exhibition.

One of the most important plaids in the collection begun by Provost Cochran, is known as 'The Chinese Fairytale Shawl'. This detail shows the exquisite workmanship of this plaid, which was probably made in France.

Provost Robert Cochran.

single gift of shawls. Mr. William McIntyre, a descendant of Provost Robert Cochran of Paisley, donated a collection which had been built up in the family over the years, beginning in the Provost's time. The collection numbered about 115 excellent examples of Paisley workmanship, many of which had very important additional information along with them. This collection was important enough to merit its own exhibition which was opened in October of that same year by the donor's sister. The following year another large collection, this time of over 45 shawls, came to the Museum from Miss Dorothy Whyte. Miss Whyte had been acting Curator of the Museum during the war years,

and she is known throughout Britain as a leading expert on the history of the shawl fashion.

In the years since 1965 there has been an average of more than sixteen shawls added to the collection each year, and the Museum is pursuing an active policy of collecting, with a particular view to filling some of the gaps in the collection as it stands. The 1970s also saw probably the most important event in the history of Paisley Museum's shawl collection.

This 1840s shawl from the Cochran family collection, still has the original handwritten label attached to the reverse side.

Printed shawl, c 1850, donated by Miss Whyte.

View of the old Shawl Gallery, taken c 1920, showing the cramped and unsuitable display conditions.

This was the opening in 1974 of a purpose-built shawl gallery, using money originally gifted by Sir Peter Coats' son Daniel in 1918. It replaced a cramped, glass-roofed gallery that was totally unsuited to a modern textile display, and it now houses probably the most comprehensive permanent display of 'Imitation Indian' patterned shawls anywhere in the world.

Shawl gallery, Paisley Museum.

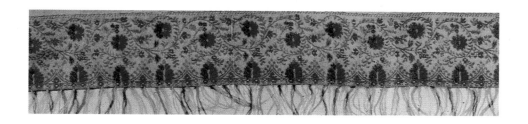

Glossary of Scottish Terms

angola	variant form of angora	*muckle*	big, much
bien	comfortable, wealthy, well-provided, plentiful	*pirn*	bobbin, fitted inside the shuttle, onto which weft is wound
brocht	brought		
bullets	a game played with round iron balls, the winner being the contestant able to hurl theirs furthest	*plides*	plaids
		poukin pin	handle by which the shuttle is pulled across the loom
carvie	caraway	*ravelins*	twisted, tangled threads
close	communal passage giving entry to several houses	*rinnin*	running
		simple	vertical cord attached to the harness which is pulled by the drawboy
close-mouth	entry to the close		
deil	a lever helping to lift the weight of the warp	*sma*	small
fash	trouble, annoy	*stent*	stretch, make taut
foucht	fought	*stumpin*	going about heavily, or clumsily
gloamin	twilight	*syne*	afterwards; *sin' syne* since then
kirk	church	*tail*	horizontal harness cord connecting the yarn to the simple
lashes	looped strings fastened so as to raise groups of warp threads simultaneously		
		tenement	large building divided into flats
lay	the part of the loom, containing the reed, which rocks back and forth to beat up the cloth	*thae*	those
		thocht	thought
		thrang	busy: a term often applied to a time or season of busy engagement or constant employment
lug	ear		
lum	chimney	*thrums*	short threads kept by a weaver for mending his web
midden	rubbish-heap, dunghill		
mid-room	single room apartment, in a tenement with three flats to a landing	*tuck*	beat (of a drum)
		whiles	sometimes

Source Material

A.H.W.C.   *Report from the Assistant Handloom Weavers' Commissioners,* Part I, 1839

Anon   'Paisley — The Shawl Trade' in *Hogg's Weekly Instructor,* November 1846

Blair   Matthew Blair, *The Paisley Shawl and the Men who Produced it,* Paisley 1904

Brown   Robert Brown, *Paisley Poets,* Paisley 1889

Clabburn 1975   Pamela Clabburn, *Norwich Shawls,* Norfolk Museums Information Sheet, 1975

Clabburn 1981   Pamela Clabburn, *Shawls,* Shire Publications, 1981

Conran   Shirley Conran 'The Persistence of Paisley' in *The Observer,* Colour Supplement, 17th October 1965

Cross   William Cross, *Changes in the Style of Paisley Shawls,* Paisley 1872

Cunnington   C.W. & P. Cunnington, *Handbook of Costume in the Nineteenth Century,* Faber and Faber, 1959

Gilmour 1871   David Gilmour, *The Pen Folk,* Paisley 1871

Gilmour 1876   David Gilmour, *Paisley Weavers of Other Days,* Paisley 1876

Hislop   George R. Hislop, *History of the Paisley Gas Undertaking,* Paisley 1915

Irwin 1966   Francina Irwin, 'Prelude to the Paisley Shawl' in *Scotland's Magazine,* February 1966

Irwin 1954   John Irwin, 'The Norwich Shawl', in *Country Life Annual,* 1954

Irwin 1973   John Irwin, *The Kashmir Shawl,* Her Majesty's Stationery Office, 1973

King   Margaret R. King, *Cashmere Shawls,* Cincinnati Museum, 1921

Leavitt   T.W. Leavitt, 'Fashion, Commerce and Technology in the Nineteenth Century: 'The Shawl Trade', in *Textile History,* Volume 3, December 1972

Lévi-Strauss   Monique Lévi-Strauss, 'Le Tissage des châles au Cachemire en France' in *La Mode du Châle Cachemire en France,* Ville de Paris Musée de la Mode et du Costume, 1982

Muir   Meta Muir, 'The Edinburgh Shawl' in *A Century of Scottish Shawlmaking,* Edinburgh Corporation Libraries and Museums Committee, 1962

P.D.E.   *Paisley Daily Express*

P.R.G.   *Paisley & Renfrewshire Gazette*

Parkhill   John Parkhill, *The History of Paisley,* Paisley, 1857

Pauly — Sarah Buie Pauly, 'The Shawl: Its Context and Construction', in *The Kashmir Shawl*, Yale University Art Gallery, 1975

Rock — C.H. Rock, *Paisley Shawls, A Chapter of the Industrial Revolution*, Paisley Museum and Art Galleries, 1966

Rothstein — Natalie Rothstein, 'The Introduction of the Jacquard Loom to Great Britain', in *Studies in Textile History*, Royal Ontario Museum, 1977

Russell — Dr. William Russell, 'Paisley Weavers of the Old School', *The Paisley and Renfrewshire Gazette*, 6th July to 3rd August 1901

S.S.A. — 'Parish of Paisley' in *The Second Statistical Account of Scotland*, Vol. No. VII, 1837

Semple — R. Semple, 'A Drawboy's Memories' in *The Paisley and Renfrewshire Gazette*, 1st July 1905

Smout — T.C. Smout, 'Paisley in Depression 1841-3' in *The Search for Wealth and Stability*, ed. T.C. Smout, Macmillan Press, 1979

Stewart 1932 — A.M. Stewart, 'Paisley Shawls: The End of the Chapter', in *Scottish Home and Country*, August 1932

Stewart 1946 — A.M. Stewart, *The History and Romance of The Paisley Shawl*, Paisley 1946

T.S.A. — 'Shawl of English Cashmeer Wool', in *Transactions of the Society of Arts*, Vol. 46, 1828

Völker — Angela Völker, 'Die Produktion von 'Wiener Shawls' in der ersten Hälfte des 19. Jahrhunderts' in *Festschrift für Sigrid Müller-Christensen*, Deutscher Kunstverlag, Munich 1981

Whyte 1949 — D.A. Whyte, *The Paisley Shawl*, Scottish Woollens No. 39, June 1949

Whyte 1974 — D.A. Whyte, 'The Makers of Paisley Shawls', Text of an address given to the Anthropology Section of the British Association at Stirling, 4th September 1974, M.S. in Paisley Museum

Whyte 1976 — D.A. Whyte, 'Edinburgh Shawls and their Makers', in *Costume*, No. 10, 1976

Wilson — John Wilson, *General View of the Agriculture of Renfrewshire*, Paisley 1812

Acknowledgements

The author gratefully acknowledges all assistance received in the matter of illustrations for this book.

'The Desborough Mirror' and 'Abdullah Qutb-Shah' are reproduced by courtesy of the Trustees of the British Museum.

'Fragment of a 17th century Kashmir shawl', 'Early 18th century "vase of flowers" style Kashmir shawl' and 'Shaul Goat from Boutan' are reproduced by courtesy of the Board of Trustees of the Victoria and Albert Museum.

The two illustrations of products at the 1851 Great Exhibition are taken from the 1970 republication of 'The Art Journal special issue Illustrated Catalogue of the Crystal Palace Exhibition London 1851', published by Dover Publications Inc., New York.

The 'native painting of a Kashmir shawl loom' is reproduced by courtesy of the India Office Library.

The 'Design registered at the Patent Office by David Sime' is reproduced by courtesy of the Public Record Office, Kew (Ref. BT 43/181, reg. no. 9391).

Other historical photographs are from the collections of Renfrew District Museums & Art Galleries Service.

New photographic work was done by Rick Beattie of Edinburgh and Jim Hermit of Glasgow.

The author also wishes to thank all the friends and colleagues with whom she has discussed the subject of Paisley shawls over the years. In particular, thanks must go to Mr. D.R. Shearer, former Chief Curator of Renfrew District Museums, for his help and encouragement from the very beginning of the project; to Jim Erskine, Design & Exhibitions Officer, without whom the book would never have been done; R.A. Saunders, Keeper of Art, for assistance with portrait material; to Mrs. A. Gibson for historical photograph research; to Sheila Begbie for initial visualisations; and last but not least to the Museum's typists for their endless patience in correcting the manuscript.

Index